Edward Reynolds Roe

God Reigns

lay sermons - Vol. 1

Edward Reynolds Roe

God Reigns
lay sermons - Vol. 1

ISBN/EAN: 9783337266035

Printed in Europe, USA, Canada, Australia, Japan

Cover: Foto ©Lupo / pixelio.de

More available books at **www.hansebooks.com**

GOD REIGNS

LAY SERMONS

BY

EDWARD REYNOLDS ROE, M. D.

CHICAGO
LAIRD & LEE Publishers
Clark and Adams Streets

GOD REIGNS

SERMON I.

"In the beginning God created the heavens and the earth."—Genesis 1: 1.

This all-comprehensive announcement is concerning GOD : not *a* God, not *some* God, not even *the* God; and not any anthropomorphized deification of man. God is without person (except as a human conception), without gender, number or tense, the same yesterday, to-day and forever. How, then, can we by searching find out God? Granted, that we cannot : a mouse in his nest at the base cannot find out a mountain ; but in his narrow house he may learn of that which is nearest in his circumscribed horizon and know that there is a mountain. We cannot by searching find out anything in its ultimate essence. We know something of electricity, of gravity, of life, of consciousness, of emotion ; but we know none of them in their ultimate. We know something of the starry heavens ; we search them with wonderful optical devices, and where these fail we penetrate still farther by the spectroscope and the photograph ; and yet while

> On forever will the thought pursue,
> The stars extend beyond forever too.

In a degree almost infinitely less than our knowledge of all those and countless other systems, may we not know God? Let us inquire :

1. As to the existence of God.—

Nowhere in the writings of Moses, or in the New Testament, is any direct attempt made to prove the existence of God ; that is and must be assumed as the basis of all reasoning. The God-sentiment, feeling the existence of God, has probably been common, in greater or less degree of crudity and grossness among all peoples. And all have agreed at least in this : that each has clothed his idol in his own human attributes ; and their gods are cruel, vengeful, jealous, dishonest, or loving, beneficent, forgiving and fatherly, after the model of their own natures. Some, however, have denied the existence of God ; but it is the God of others they deny, while themselves deify Nature, or Law, or even Chance. But the God-sentiment toward the great controlling and unifying Harmony of the universe remains, even with them who have expelled God from their reason.

The existence of God, then, is assumed, and is admitted to be in the nature of things as incapable of proof as is that of the universe. Berkeley, and many other philosophers before him and since, and many of them in a more absolute manner than he, have denied the existence of matter ; but whether objectively in itself or subjectively in ourselves only, matter exists to all men. Let it be only in the foci of forces, or existent in substantial atoms, men will continue to believe in its existence though they continue to dispute as to its essence. So of the existence and attributes of God.

2. Of God's Infinity.—

It is granted that we can have no comprehension of infinity, but we may think of that which we cannot comprehend. We may think of illimitable space: we cannot comprehend it; though from the nature of the human mind we cannot feel otherwise than that space must be infinite. Indeed, space is nothing, and cannot be limited or bounded. We may think of illimitable time, but we cannot comprehend it, for time in itself, like space, is nothing. But as our mental organization offers us the conception of duration, we may think of its unending continuance. In the same manner, we must come to have a conception—not a comprehension—of the infinity of God.

3. Of God's Personality.—

To deny the personality of God is admitted heterodoxy. But what is personality? Does not the answer depend on the degree of mental culture in him who answers? To think of God as having characteristics of personality is to endow the conception with form and bounding limits, as of a man. But that is surely a very crude conception, wholly incompatible with that of an infinite God, without limit and everywhere present; and it may well be questioned whether any who have thought deeply on these things have really any such conception as that.

But there is a sense in which the personality of God may reasonably be conceived, just as the child personifies SANTA CLAUS, or as men personify HAMLET, Othello, or other creations of genius.

But the personification of God becomes less definite and personal as men rise in their conception of his character, until all thought of outline and form disappear, and God appears as the All-in-all of the universe.

At this point a very curious question arises: May there be more than one universe? Space being illimitable, there is room for any number of universes, not interfering with and totally disconnected with each other. In the visible universe, as we are told by astronomers, there are indications of a region which is central as to the suns and systems reached by our telescopes; is there also a circumference as well as a center? Then why not other universes without number in the infinite space? But these are vain questions which can never be answered.

4. Of the Immanency of God in all things.—

The Hebrew psalmist in his conception of the omnipresence of God had reached far beyond the grossness so common in his day. "Whither shall I go from thy spirit? or whither shall I fly from Thy presence? If I ascend into heaven, Thou art there; If I make my bed in hell, behold thou art there. If I take the wings of the morning and dwell in the uttermost parts of the sea, even there shall Thy hand guide me and Thy right hand shall hold me." [Psalm cxxxix, 7.] But God's omnipresence must be assumed as inseparable from any reasonable conception of the All-father. What is here to be briefly considered is the inherent, in-dwelling, constituting, sustaining, controlling Wisdom, Power and Love of God in all things. And this profound and all-comprehensive doctrine is to be taken as the central harmony of the universe; so that the unity of God implies the harmonious and consistent unity of all things.

As to the manifestation of this unity in the visible universe, our knowledge is much greater now than was deemed possible half a century since. By use of the spectroscope we have traced the elements of our earth and the chemical laws of their action and interaction to the sun, the comets and the central suns of other systems; by the photograph we have followed the chemical effects of light beyond the reach of the telescope to invisible stars; aerolites falling to the earth from the sun, the moon, the star-dust of interstellar space, disintegrated comets or ruined worlds — whencesoever they may come—have answered the chemist's quest with elements of the earth, subject to the same chemical laws; while to the astronomer's eye the myriad shining worlds and wandering comets and careering meteors all move to the harmonious rhythm of a single system of celestial mechanics.

Everywhere are the evidences of unity, and to the devout mind, everywhere the evidence of the immanency of God, who is proclaimed by Moses to have "created the heavens and the earth," and "in whom we live and move and have our being."

We are to consider then, not that God is above and beyond and apart from the universe, sending forth edict and decree for its government, but that God's intimate presence is the essential existence of all things, without which there is neither matter nor force, neither thought nor feeling, neither life nor organization.

All the forces which control the physical universe, all the feelings which move in the moral and emotional, are but manifestations of the in-dwelling power and love of God; all the mysteries of the moving heavens, the synthetic relations of material atoms and the unending miracles of organization and life are only the utterance of the wisdom of God.

5. Of Consciousness as an Attribute of God.

Having now very briefly referred to the existence, infinity, personality and immanency of God in all things, and before proceeding to the consideration of God's consciousness, note that up to this point there is no dispute; all men who have thought upon the subject admit the existence of a universe, its unity, harmony and all-prevailing and undeviating laws, though they may still not admit in them the thought of the wisdom or love of God.

But as these discourses are to consider God as the sum and substance of all things, it became necessary to state the foregoing definitions as the foundation stones of the entire series, without which no intelligible structure of thought could be built. But the chief corner stone of that structure is intended to be the *consciousness* of that infinite existence which some call "Law," or "Nature,"—GOD, who "created the heavens and the earth."

What is consciousness? The American lexicographer defines it as "The knowledge of what passes in our own mind." That is human consciousness. It must be almost infinitely below that consciousness which appears to pervade the universe. Man's consciousness is the knowledge of his own thought, the internal perception of his own reasoning. But does the universe as a whole or in any operation of nature or of natural law indicate reason? Perhaps not reason after the human pattern. Reason is not the highest attribute of man—though usually so esteemed—but love, unselfish, spontaneous, unexacting love toward all conscious and sentient creatures, men and animals, without the hope or expectation of return, or any question of worthiness in the recipient. Reason is but the conscious operation of mental gropings after truth not manifest to direct perception. We never reason in pursuit of that we know, but of that we do not otherwise perceive. It is only a kind of mental mechanism, like a calculating machine, by which we reach the unknown through the interdependence of known premises. Could we perceive all truth, possess all knowledge through our powers of observation alone, all reasoning would be at an end.

It would appear therefore that reason is not predicable of God, knowing all things from the beginning. While, then, wisdom is an attribute of God, it is not the wisdom of reason but of infinite knowledge, the same yesterday, to-day and forever.

And while, then, God does not reason after the method of man, we must still conceive of God's infinite consciousness, embracing the whirling suns and systems and the movement of infinitesimal atoms.

Does God, then, hear and see, as well as know? "He that planted the ear, shall he not hear? He who formed the eye shall he not see?" Yes, in a sense beyond our comprehension God must hear and see; and in the same incomprehensible manner to the human mind, are exerted all the volitions of the Divine mind. And while we may see and appreciate some of these, as "seen through a glass darkly," it must be always under the limitations of our own finite minds, out of which must come our imperfect conceptions of the infinite.

6. Of the Will of God.

The Will and the Power of God are to be understood as one, as manifested in that emanant Volition by which all things are controlled and sustained. It is that which by them who deny God is called Law, or Nature, or Force, and which by those unbelievers is supposed to be without consciousness and volition.

What, then, is to be understood by the declaration that " In the beginning God created the heavens and the earth?" Manifestly this: that from the beginning they have existed by the emanant Volition of God,—that is, from the beginning of these heavens and this earth, which modern science admits to have been within a limited period of time, no matter how vast. But more than this, writers of the Old Testament and of the New held that since that indefinite " beginning," God's wisdom and power have created, controlled and upheld all things as in the beginning. So that the statement in Genesis is only an indefinite limitation in time applicable to "the heavens and the earth" for the grand announcement that their creator is God. And Moses in the beginning of Genesis, and with that grand simplicity of statement which is unparalleled, exhibits the continuous creative power of God through all evolutions of advancement upon the earth down to the era of mankind.

In what way, then, does the Divine volition become efficient? The answer is : We do not and cannot know. We do not know how our own will secures its behests in the control of our own bodies and its organs. But we may know, up to certain limits, what in the past has been the rule of action in the manifestation of divine power. In the movements of the heavenly bodies that manifestation we have called *gravity* and inertia, and we have learned the mode and sequence in which they appear always to secure the observed results ; but who shall say how gravity disposes all matter to come together, or how inertia determines all bodies to maintain unchanged their present condition of comparative rest or motion ? the accustomed modes in which these results occur—their rule of action—we call Natural Laws; but the law is only the rule of action: the power behind is God,—at once the legislative, judicial and executive power. We know the modes in which *affinity* operates in the synthesis and analysis of simple and compound bodies from elementary atoms; the sum of these modes we call chemistry. But who knows how affinity operates in assuring its results and those modes of action which we cite as the laws of chemical force? We are beginning to know much as to the manner in which life determines organization, and many of the manifold mysteries of plants and animals; but what do we know of life itself? Nothing, not even whether it is the antecedent or consequence of organization.

In all these things we can only know results, and the sequences according to which they occur—their modes of action—and we call these modes natural laws. But God is behind all, in all and over all.

7. Of God's love.—

The Apostle John declares, absolutely, that " God *is* Love."—1st Gen'l Epist. IV, 7.

Many of the Old Testament writers, and

especially David in the Psalms, proclaim the Love of God, notwithstanding the vengeful aspect of the Hebrew theology; and Love is almost the entire burden of the teachings of Jesus, who consented to a terrible death for his love to men. David exclaims: "How excellent is thy loving kindness, Oh God! therefore the children of men put their trust under the shadow of thy wings." [Psalm xxvi, 7]. And Jesus in the Sermon on the mount, declares that the love of God is absolute and without conditions: "I say unto you, Love your enemies and pray for them that persecute you, that ye may be sons of your Father which is in heaven: for he maketh his sun to rise on the evil and the good, and sendeth rain on the just and the unjust." [Matt. vi, 44]. And he declares that it was also the law as announced by Moses, and one of the Commandments, that "thou shalt love thy neighbor as thyself," [Matt. xix, 19], not teaching that man's love should be more unconditional than that of God, but the same.

It is to be understood then, that the love of God which is "over all his works," is infinite and without reserve toward all his creatures, and unqualified by their acts, whether good or evil. But this does not conflict with the declaration that "Whom the Lord loveth he chasteneth," [Heb. xii, 6], for in the very nature of things it is impossible to receive the happiness involved in the law of our being, except by conformity therewith.

In this series of discourses it is to be admitted, then, that to them who do not accept the Bible as a direct revelation from God, his existence and attributes can only be shown in the same manner as that of the so-called natural laws, which we know only from their observed effects; and in the same manner as the existence of gravity, inertia, affinity and the laws of life and organization are assumed in the Godless treatises of modern science, it is intended to replace God as the supreme head of the universe, physical, mental and moral.

SERMON II.

"And the Spirit of God moved upon the face of the waters."—Gen. 1, 2.

An amusement not uncommon among lads of an inquiring turn of mind consists in setting on end a hundred bricks to see the whole series successively fall from an impulse given to the first. It may be taken as a not inapt illustration of modern physical philosophy. Push the first brick with the hand and the energy thereby imparted over-comes the inertia of rest and changes it to the inertia of motion: it is now disposed to move, and passing beyond the centre of gravity, it falls against the second .of the series from the joint effects of the original muscular impulse, gravity and its own inertia. Striking the second of the series, it imparts to that a portion of its own inertia of motion—its momentum— and impels it to strike the third in the series from the movement transmitted from the first. In the same manner the third is made to overthrow the fourth, and so in succession to the end of the series.

Now the theory of all this is: the whole series of bricks from the disposition common to all bodies to maintain that condition of rest or of motion in which they may at any time be found, being now at rest, would remain so forever, unless a disposition to move be imparted from without. Gravitation toward the earth's centre being in equilibrium on all sides, maintains them in the upright position, and their inertia disposes them to remain at rest. But when the first of the series receives an impulse from without, it falls, and the sequential fall of the whole follows by the transmission to the last of the impulse imparted to the first, in accordance with the "laws of Motion." As stated by Newton these are:

1. Every body continues in its state of rest or uniform motion in a straight line, unless compelled to change the state by an external force.

2. Every motion or change of motion is in direction of the force impressed and is proportionate to it.

3. Action and reaction are equal, and opposite in direction.

Since Newton's time some additional laws have been discovered which may affect motion, the most essential of which is known as that of the "Correlation and Conservation of Force," or more correctly as now held, the "Conservation of Energy." It is stated thus:

"Considering the universe as a whole, the *sum* of all forces is a constant quantity." According to this doctrine energy is as indestructible as matter. But all energy may be changed in *form* and converted from one to another, so as to appear as mechanical energy of motion, heat, light, electricity, chemical affinity and (as held by some) muscular contractility, etc. And of these *motion* is considered the essential basis, and the varieties of force but modes of motion. And these and other so-called natural laws are held to be sufficient to account for the universe as it has been in the past, now is and ever shall be. Many prominent scientists hold that there never was any first cause of matter and of worlds and all that in them is, neither in a beginning as relates to time, nor any present relation of causation; and some deny the existence of any cause at any time, and hold that the only relation between events is that of sequence, one thing following another in an infinite series of sequences. According to these no intelligent volition moved the first of nature's bricks, no conscious energy set them up, and they fell not from any true causation, but only from inevitable sequence by which the first brick of a series becomes the antecedent of the second, and so through the series, backward as well as forward. And they hold that the number of bricks necessary to illustrate their views is infinite and not to be counted by hundreds, and that they have received an infinite number of impulses down to the present time, and will transmit them to other bricks *ad infinitum*, either as mechanical motion, heat, light, electricity or some other mode of the common sum of energy in the universe. Now, suppose we withdraw the consciousness controlling the arm of the boy who erects his hundred bricks and starts them to knocking each other down; is there any possible operation of any form of energy known to science which can set up the hundred bricks and start them again to falling one by one, without the intervention of intelligent volition? It is safe to assert that there is not. And yet, independent of any series of sequences connecting him with what follows, the lad by his will, guided by his intelligence, sets in motion the muscular contractions which erect the series and start the first brick, and insure the effects of gravitation and inertia in upsetting the whole number. Could the establishment of the solar system and the fitting up of the earth and all the wonders of nature be accomplished without intelligent volition, and yet *not* the setting up and the knocking down of a hundred bricks? How much greater must be the credulity required to believe that than the declaration of Moses: "In the beginning God created the heavens and the earth?"

It is not denied that the procedure of evolution in the history of the solar system and of the earth has been according to ascertained natural laws, but only the efficiency of the laws themselves in inducing and determining the results. And it will be maintained in these discourses that the universe is controlled by a conscious and constant volition upon which the so-called laws themselves depend. John in the Gospel bearing his name, declares: "God is a spirit," [IV, 24]; but they who pretend to understand the laws of nature are unable to understand what spirit is—and very naturally; but how then do they understand what the law of gravitation is, which extends and operates invisibly throughout the universe? Paul told the men of Athens that "God made the world and all things therein," and that they should "seek God, if haply they might feel after him and find him, though he is not far from each one of us." [Acts XVII, 27]. Is it any more difficult to conceive of the presence of God in all things than that of gravity? We know of gravitation only by its effects; may we not know God in the same way? But gravity, we are told, is a law of matter; but no one explains how it operates to produce the observed effects, or can determine whether it resides in matter or operates from without. It is mysterious as God, and its existence no more certainly proven. So with other "laws of nature," the operation of which produces results so like those of intelligent volition as to leave no reasonable doubt that the laws themselves are only the rules of action under which that volition operates.

Leading scientists now-a-days write for the

eyes of each other more than for the general public; and it is the fashion among them to ignore God, and never to mention his name, —some because they deny him, and some because, as they say, nothing can be known concerning him. But no men since the days of Jesus and his apostles have, though unwittingly, done so much to demonstrate the existence of God (to them who are able to receive it) as these same doubting scientists, who recite the history of creation from the original star-dust down to the present time totally oblivious of God. With some additions they admit as a beginning the well known nebular hypothesis first propounded by Laplace; which briefly stated was this: It supposed the matter of the solar system to have "existed originally in the form of a vast diffused revolving nebula, which gradually cooling and contracting, threw off, in obedience to mechanical and physical laws, successive rings of matter, from which subsequently by the same laws were produced the several planets, satelites and other bodies of the system." And by these same laws, and certain others equally without intelligence, it is now held, that the earth and its inhabitants have originated and reached their present condition.

In 1874, at Belfast, Ireland, Professor John Tyndall, one of the ablest and most candid, and certainly the most eloquent of British scientists, in reviewing this whole subject said:

"Abandoning all disguise, the confession that I feel bound to make to you is, that I prolong the vision backward across the boundary of the experimental evidence, and discern in that matter which we in our ignorance, and notwithstanding our professed reverence for its Creator, have hitherto covered with opprobrium the promise and potency of every form and quality of life."

Now, this declaration implies, either that Prof. Tyndall by his backward vision in the original nebula of star-dust saw sufficient potency and promise of the earth's beginning and progress down to the present hour without either love or intelligence, or that he saw the intelligence and love in the laws themselves by which the results have been secured.

If the former alternative was his belief, then he must claim that the laws from which love and wisdom are absent have insured results which so resemble those of intelligent volition as to make its absence more difficult to demonstrate than the existence of God ; or he must claim that the laws of nature are themselves endowed with the attributes of Deity. Why not say at once that God is the source of the natural laws, and so save much circumlocution?

In defending himself against certain criticisms in the "Contemporary Review" of his utterances in this Belfast address, Prof. Tyndall said :

"It is a matter of experience that an earthly father, who is at the same time both wise and tender, listens to the requests of his children, and if they do not ask amiss, takes pleasure in granting their requests. We know also that this compliance extends to the alteration, within certain limits of the current of events on earth. With this suggestion offered by our experience, it is no departure from scientific method to place behind natural phenomena a universal Father, who, in answer to the prayers of his children alters the currents of those phenomena. * * * The conception of personal volition in nature is suggested by the ordinary action of man upon earth." But he claims that this has not been proven, and declares that "without *verification* a theoretic conception is a mere figment of the intellect."

There are some very remarkable admissions in these paragraphs for a scientist who believes matter and law to be all-sufficient in explaining the phenomena of the earth and its living inhabitants.

1. It is admitted that even the volition of men may alter the current of natural phenomena, without destroying the harmony of the universe, as many claim that would do. If, then, the infinite series of sequences can be thus harmlessly broken by the will of men, much more must that sequence be subject to infinite intelligence and power, safely secured against injury by infinite love. But the admission that the current of natural phenomena may be changed by any power whatever is not the belief of other materialistic teachers, as will be shown hereafter.

2. It is admitted to be "no departure from scientific method to place behind natural phenomena a universal Father" who "alters the currents of those phenomena." It is some

relief to learn from so eminent authority that belief in God is not unscientific, even though it may be unverified and therefore "a mere figment of the intellect." But how about the "universal ether" which is claimed by men of science to fill all space, even permeating all known bodies, and forming the connecting medium between all worlds? It is not pretended that its existence can be verified; it is assumed as a necessity to explain known facts in nature. And though the whole frame of modern science would fall without it, it must be, until verified, "a mere figment of the intellect." It is equally true of the "Atomic Theory" accepted as the basis of chemical science. The existence of atoms has not been and probably cannot be verified. So with some other theoretic conceptions admitted by scientists, the assumption of which is less logical than to "place God behind the phenomena of nature," as expressed by Prof. Tyndall.

On the whole, the most remarkable thing about this address is, that admitting so much, Mr. Tyndall did not feel impelled to admit more, and then and there announce his belief in a conscious Will and an infinite loving kindness over all the universe.

It would in the present state of science be hardly worth while to enquire whether Moses meant to declare that God created the heavens and the earth out of nothing, or that he made them by the power of conscious volition out of previously existing matter, because it is now a debated question whether there really is any such thing as matter, in the old sense of any substance which occupies space. Some now hold that what has been called material atoms are but focal centres of natural forces; and others that our conceptions of material things are subjective and arise within, and do not exist as objects without, as they appear to us. But in any case, Moses intended to teach that God by infinite wisdom, love and power, controlled and determined the evolution of the earth, from the original chaos down to the coming of man and after; and that " God saw everything that he had made, and behold, it was very good!"

In so far then as the exceedingly small may illustrate the infinitely great, the child's amusement with the hundred bricks may illustrate the creation of the heavens and the earth. Infinite volition set up and overset as the divine plan demanded, the elements which have entered into the creation of the universe, the fitting up of the earth for the habitation of sentient creatures, and culminating at last in the coming of man.

It is not a little remarkable that the account over three thousand years ago given by Moses, instructed, as was said by Stephen [Acts VII: 27], "in all the wisdom of the Egyptians," should so nearly correspond with that given by modern astronomers and geologists. The science known to the Egyptians, if Moses had his knowledge from that, was much more advanced than has generally been believed, as to the cosmogony and successive peopling of the earth by plants, fishes, birds, mammals and man. And if Moses did not learn his cosmogony from the Egyptians, it must be asked of him as was done of one greater than Moses: "Whence hath this man these things?" [Mark VI: 2].

As to the indefinite evenings and mornings alluded to by Moses, there appears sufficient room to believe they have been as long as the vast periods claimed by the astronomers and geologists, and gave ample time for the development of results in accordance with the course of those natural laws so much relied upon by some leaders in science who teach that Nature is able, if only we allow time enough, to get along without God.

In conclusion for this hour, it is perhaps safe to assume that whether from the teachings of Moses, from beholding the wonderful works of divine power and loving kindness, or from the sentiment of worship which is inwrought in the human heart, men will continue to exclaim with the Psalmist : " Oh, Lord, our Lord, how excellent is thy name in all the earth." [Psalms VIII: 1].

SERMON III.

"And God saw everything that he had made, and behold, it was very good."—Gen. 1, 31.

Most recent teachers of geology avoid all attempt to show any indications of intelligence as manifested in the earth's changes throughout the grand sweep of geological progress; and many of them deny that there are any such indications. The once celebrated "Bridgwater Treatise," of Buckland, prepared for the express purpose of demonstrating love and design in the earth's history, though exceedingly able, was written at a time when the science of geology was in its infancy, and is now little known. But even the citation of that interesting volume clearly indicates that if Prof. Tyndall, armed with all the scientific lore he now possesses, had been required to "prolong his vision" *forward*, instead of backward, standing at the dawn of life upon the earth, he would *not* have discerned " the promise and potency of every form and quality of life" which was to follow in the coming ages. His vision backward is better than his or any other man's vision forward. And the knowledge which we now have of the grand phenomena of the earth's evolution, "as seen across the boundary of the experimental evidence," prompts the exclamation: If "the undevout astronomer is mad," with ten-fold force must also be the undevout geologist.

But who shall condense the vast cycles of geologic history to the compass of a single discourse; and, in the language of Tyndall, "place behind the natural phenomena a universal Father?" Happy is he who has so far mastered this science of sciences as to be able in the mind's eye to behold in the grand march of the ages by which the earth has passed from the dominion of inconceivable heat, through the formation of the azoic rocks; through the paleozoic eons of progression, after organization and life appeared,—the eras of the reign of fishes, of saurians, of birds, of mammals, and the grand climax, of man. But still happier is he who is able to see in all these progressive mutations the accumulated proofs that God created the heavens and the earth, and "his tender mercies are over all His works." [Psalms CXLV, 9.]

If we deny the dominance of conscious volition and love in nature, we are compelled to assume that matter is divine. Let us see:

All matter is subject to the law of gravitation, which is thus defined: "Every particle of matter in the universe has an attraction for—tends to approach—every other particle." It is in its action instantaneous throughout the universe. Says a text-book on Natural Philosophy (Avery's): "Light and electricity require time to traverse space; not so with this force (gravitation). If a new star were created in distant space, its light might not reach the earth for hundreds of thousands of years. It might be invisible for many generations to come, but its *pull* (from gravitation) would be felt by the earth in the twinkling of an eye." But this filling of infinite space, with infinite power to act on the instant throughout all space is an attribute of Deity; and when considered closely can only be conceived of as the divine volition. But we are told by those who oppose this view that gravitation is simply a universal law of matter. But this is putting a word for an explanation: Does the so-called law fill all space and compel the obedience of matter to the law? Then it is in the nature of an infinite executive volition. Or does the gravitating tendency reside in matter itself? Then it must have infinite power of acting where it is not,—which is absurd. Sir Isaac Newton, who first defined the law of gravitation, wrote to Bentley as follows: "That gravity should be innate, inherent and essential to matter, so that one body may act upon another at a distance through a *vacuum*, and without mediation of anything else by and through this action and force may be conveyed, is to me so great an absurdity that I believe no man who has in philosophical matters a competent faculty of thinking can never fall into it." [Quoted by Lewes, "Problems of Life and Mind," Volume II, Appendix C.]

This subject has been discussed here, when we are about to consider the geological history of the earth, because gravitation is the prime agent in all its changes. Gravitation threw down upon the central focus of attraction the nebulous matter which constituted the sun and planets (including the earth), evolved the sun's heat by the law of the correlation of energy, and the central heat of the earth, which has played so important a part in its history, and so furnished the initial point in all that play of forces which marked the earth's career down to the advent of life upon the planet, and, as some contend, including that also. January 21st of this year (1887), Prof. Sir William Thompson, in a lecture at the theater of the Royal Institution, as reported by the London *Telegraph*, said: "But in the millions of years which geology carried us back, it might safely be said there must have been great changes. How had the solar fires been maintained during those ages? The scientific answer to this question was the theory of Helmholtz, that the sun was a vast globe gradually cooling, but as it cooled, shrinking, and that the shrinkage—which was the effect of gravity upon its mass—kept up the temperature. The total of the sun's heat was equal to that which would be required to keep up 476,000 millions of millions horsepower, or about 78,000 horse-power for every square metre—a little more than a square yard—and yet the modern dynamical theory of heat shows that the sun's mass would require only to fall in or contract thirty-five metres per annum to keep up that tremendous energy. At this rate the solar radius in 2,000 years' time would be about one-hundredth per cent. less than at present. * * * * *

Sir William Thompson declined to discuss any chemical source of heat, which, whatever its effect when primeval elements first came into contact, was absolutely insignificant compared with the effects of gravity after globes like the sun and the earth had been formed.

In all these speculations they were in the end driven to the ultimate elements of matter—to the question—when they thought what became of all the sun's heat—what is the luminiferous ether that fills space, and to that most wonderful form of force upon which Faraday spent so much of the thought of his later years—gravity."

So, then, gravitation is not subject to space, time, or change, and is the initial mode in all the correlations of energy. But matter is credited with another quality almost or quite as important; and though bearing a negative name—inertia—is of an exceedingly positive character. So far as we know, all the matter in the universe is moving, and rest is only relative. The law of inertia is: *Matter is incapable of changing its condition of motion, and resists any change with a force proportionate to its mass.* It will be seen that this property is in direct conflict with gravitation; and it is logical to presume that if it resides in matter, gravitation does not. We have seen that matter is unable to alter its condition of motion; but gravitation is able to alter it; and if both are attributes of matter, it involves the absurdity that matter cannot change its condition of motion, and matter can change its condition of motion.

But, however all this may be, gravity and inertia have been the chief of the modes of energy which have governed the evolution of the earth down to the present time. Then, if we are ready to "place God behind the phenomena of nature," we can see *how* the earth began its history, begotten of the fire emerging from the generative force of gravitation, with "the promise and potency of every form and quality of life."

In its earlier periods the earth must have

been in a fluid condition, and disposed to cool into a homogeneous globular mass, with water and the atmosphere equally distributed over its surface. Moses, in language adapted to the Hebrew people of his day, declares: "God said, let the waters be gathered together into one place, and let the dry land appear, and it was so." [Genesis 1, 9.]

It is almost inconceivable that by the unguided action alone of gravitation and inertia this separation could have been produced in the manner it has been, instead of leaving the ocean evenly distributed over the surface as the atmosphere is; and yet those forces are the prime factors in the earth's economy and adaptation to plants and animals, for they are the initials of heat, liquifaction, evaporation, precipitation, the upheaval of mountains and the ocean tides. "It is no departure from scientific method" (in the words of Tyndall) "to place behind the natural phenomena, a universal Father," who may use the force of gravitation as the minister of his will.

We have now seen what gravitation and inertia as prime ministers of God could effect in preparing a world for the introduction of living creatures, plants and animals. Life, the very breath of the Most High, was to exhibit its miracles, first in the waters and afterward upon the land which stood out of the waters.

It is no more possible to define Life than to define God; in a sense they are one. But its manifestation in plants and animals is specific, and must be so considered. But it is not necessary to object to certain views of Haeckel, the noted author of "The History of Creation," and a leading teacher of one of the forms of Materialism. When treating of the "unity of organic and inorganic nature," he says: "The idea of the unity of organic and inorganic nature is now firmly established. * * * The unity of all nature, the animating of all matter, the inseparability of mental power and corporeal substance. Gœthe has asserted in the following words: 'Matter can never exist and be active without mind, nor can mind without matter.'" [Volume I, page 22, "History of Creation."]

Very well. Matter was exceedingly active in forming the earth and fitting it up for plants and animals, for vast ages, before there was feeling, or cousciousness, or any manifestation of mind upon the globe, except that of the mind of God, working by gravitation and correlated forces, until the coming of plants and animals. But Haeckel claims that *all* natural bodies are equally animated. He says: "We thus arrive at the extremely important conviction that *all natural bodies* which are known to us are *equally animated*, that the distinction which has been made between animate and inanimate bodies does *not* exist when a stone is thrown into the air and falls to earth, according to definite laws, or when in a solution of salt a crystal is formed, the phenomenon is neither more nor less than a mechanical manifestation of *life* than the growth and flowering of plants, than the propagation of animals or the activity of their senses, than the perception or the formation of thought in man." [Volume I, page 23.]

Very well again. There is a good deal of theism in these views, after all. But instead of calling the author of those manifestations God, he calls him Life. Moses understood that life was but the spirit (or breath) of the Almighty, who "breathed into his" (Adam's) "nostrils the breath of life, and he became a living soul." [Genesis II, 7.] And Job declares: "The spirit of God has made me, and the breath of the Almighty hath given me life. [XXXIII, 4.]

The objection to the view of Haeckel is that it banishes consciousness from the phenomena of nature and leaves the universe indebted to gravitation as the universal bond which secures that unity which he advocates. For denying God and disregarding the mystical *ether* which is "without verification," and therefore, in the words of Tyndall, "a mere figment of the intellect," there is nothing else which fills all space and is independent of time and space.

The introduction of life upon the earth was a very slow and a very long process. Mr. Lewes, treating of the beginnings of life, says: "The conclusion seems inevitable that whereever and whenever the state of things permitted that peculiar combination of elements known as organized substance, there and then a center was established—Life had a root. From roots closely resembling each other in all essential characters, but all more or less different, there have been developed the various stems of the great tree. Myriads of roots have probably perished without issue; myriads have developed into forms so ill adapted to sustain the fluctuations of the medium, so ill-fitted for the struggle of existence, that they became extinct before even our organic record begins; myriads have become extinct since then; and the descendants of these which now survive are like the shattered regiments and companies after some terrific battle." ["Physical Basis of Mind," page 121.]

Haeckel declares that "at a certain definite time life had its beginnings upon earth, and that terrestrial organisms did not exist from eternity, but at a certain period came into existence for the first time." [History of Creation, Volume I, page 337.]

How was life—living organisms—introduced upon the earth? " At this point," says Haeckel, "most naturalists, even at the present day, are inclined to give up the attempt at natural explanation, and take refuge in the miracle of an inconceivable creation." And yet this same philosopher details the steps of that stupendous miracle in which he himself believes, the evolution of man from a sponge. What does he do with the problem of life's origin upon the earth? He falls back on the exploded hypothesis of *spontaneous generation*— the derivation of the living from the not-living. He labors through a dozen pages to prove the *possibility* of spontaneous or parentless generation; admits that it has not been shown, and rests in the declaration that "the impossibility of such a process can never be proved." And, "if we do not accept this hypothesis of spontaneous generation," he concludes, "then at this one point of the history of development we must have recourse to the miracle of a supernatural creation. The Creator must have created the first organism, or a few first organisms, from which all others are derived." [History of Creation, Volume I, page 343.]

No, there is no such alternative. Replace God "behind the phenomena of nature," as Tyndall says; or better, restore Him to His kingdom *amid* the phenomena of nature, and no miracle is needed—or all is miracle, at all times. It need not be conceived that God interposes from without, like a wise king ruling his dominions, but only that he works his will within the phenomena of the universe. Nor is it to be supposed that the divine mind ponders upon his acts, after the manner of men who, not knowing all things, must consider of them by their reason. God, who knoweth all things from the beginning, needs not to reason, nor to plan, nor to have any designs for the future; and he enacts no miracles which involve the violation of His own laws—that is of His order and unchangeableness. God and His universe are as harmonious in their operation as the functions of a living organism. He does not set a universal mechanism to running, and leave it to take care of itself. He constantly "upholds all things by the word of His power." [Hebrews 1, 3.]

How living beings were introduced upon the earth—the mechanical or philosophical manner of their origin and genesis,—is unknown, and will probably forever remain so. One thing appears now to be settled beyond peradventure: All living creatures now existing were derived from previously existing living parents. It is also no longer questioned that life upon the earth had a beginning, ages after the planet had formed a hardened crust upon the central mass. But at what definite geological epoch life first appeared is not clearly ascertained; for living creatures may have lived, died, become fossilized, and afterward melted down in the igneous rocks before the earliest forms still preserved to us came into existence. But the exceeding simplicity of the fossil organisms which are still preserved in the oldest fossiliferous rocks indicates that we have reached back in our researches almost to the beginning of life on the globe.

And now, when we consider the introduction of living organisms upon the earth, it must appear to us the most stupendous event in the history of the universe.

According to evolutionists, a few specks of protoplasmic albumen, having been not alive, suddenly lived, multiplied themselves by dividing into countless millions, were evolved into living nucleated cells, which were aggregated into more and more complex organisms, as shown by geology—fishes, reptiles, mammals, man—following each other at inconceivable periods of time in the geological history. Organized manifestations of God, expressing, in infinitely lower degree — feeling, sensation, perception, volition, consciousness, righteousness, love.

Before the coming of living creatures neither feeling, sensation, perception, volition, consciousness, reason, righteousness nor love had any receptacles upon the earth, and no organisms by which they might be manifested or received. Gravitation and inertia as ministers of His providential power had formed the earth into a proper habitation for the coming recipients of God's love and wisdom; and advancing organization and the rise of feeling, perception, volition, consciousness, reason, righteousness, and love—the most God-like of all—moved on together. Well might David exclaim: "The works of the Lord are great, sought out of all them that have pleasure in them. His work is honorable and glorious, and his righteousness endureth forever." [Psalms CXI, 2, 3.]

SERMON IV.

"And God said: Let the waters bring forth abundantly the moving creature that hath life, and fowl that may fly above the earth in the open firmament of heaven. And God said: Let the earth bring forth the living creature after his kind, cattle and creeping things, and beasts of the earth after his kind; and it was so."—Gen. I, 20, 24.

We have now to consider the sweeping hypothesis which has interfered with all religious creeds and all philosophies—the hypothesis of evolution. And in the very beginning it becomes necessary to define, as near as may be in a single discourse, the most comprehensive system of philosophy ever maintained. Evolutionists are far from being agreed among themselves as to the less important points of their system; but the following statement is believed to recite the fundamental propositions upon which nearly all teachers of evolution agree:

1. The material laws of the universe, without the interposition of God, have brought the sun, the planets and the earth from chaotic nebula or star-dust to their present condition.

2. That other natural laws—or correlations of the same—have introduced living creatures, plants and animals, upon the earth.

3. That the first living things were simply formless specks of albuminous matter, which had been not-living, and were parentless.

4. That those living amorphous specks of protoplasmic albumin, few in number at first, multiplied themselves by division into countless millions, increased through successive eras the complexity of their forms and functions until, in the course of measureless ages they had evolved successively highly organized plants, and improved animal organisms—fishes, saurians, birds, mammals, man and all intermediate forms and modes of life.

In explanation and support of these propositions, evolutionists rely upon the following agencies, assumed to be mechanical and self-acting natural laws:

1. The "Struggle for Existence," as it is called by Darwin; or, the "Competition for

the Means of Subsistence," as Haeckel terms it; who also declares that "Darwin assumes no kind of unknown forces of nature, nor hypothetical conditions, as the acting causes for the *transformation* of organic forms, but solely and simply the universally recognized vital activities of all organisms, which we term inheritance and adaptation." That "the interaction of these two functions effects a continual, slow transmutation of organic forms is," he declares, "a necessary result of the struggle for existence." [History of Creation, Volume 1, page 169.]

Again, he says: "All the different forms of organisms which people are usually inclined to look upon as the products of a creative power, acting for a definite purpose, we, according to the Theory of Selection, can conceive as the necessary productions of natural selection, working without a purpose—as the unconscious interaction between the two properties of mutability and hereditivity." [History of Creation, Volume 1, page 176.]

In that never-ending struggle, the weaker and least adapted to their environments, perish early, while the stronger and better adapted survive and conform themselves by physiological action more and more to their surroundings, modifying both forms and functions.

These *adaptations* and *survival of the fittest* are the first steps in the evolution of new species of plants and animals.

2. The transmission to offspring by inheritance of those modified forms and adaptations accumulated from generation to generation, giving rise to new species by "Natural Selection," or "What is the same thing," says Haeckel, "by the interaction of *Inheritance* and *Adaptation* in the struggle for life."

3. New functions and new forms of the organs arise according to "the law of cumulative adaptations and established inheritance;" and so, it is maintained, all complex forms have arisen, including organs of the senses and the mental faculties of man, by the progressive adaptation of the brain; and including the moral sentiments, as insisted by Mr. Herbert Spencer in his book entitled "The Data of Ethics." And all this without any intelligent purpose or control.

The question to be examined is—not the truth of the evolutionary history of the earth and its inhabitants as recited by teachers of the new philosophy: science will finally decide all questions of that kind, but—have those changes by which formless lumps of not-living albumen lived, and from which man is declared to have been evolved, come about without the intervention of conscious volition? Has the universe been evolved from chaotic matter without the controlling will of God? Haeckel, and most evolutionists, reply in the affirmative; and as the great German scholar and evolutionist makes, perhaps, the clearest statement of that side of the question, frequent reference will be made in this discussion to the English edition of his "History of Creation."

It appears to be at present fully established that living plants and animals do not now come into existence in any other manner than by descent from living parents; life does not spontaneously arise. It is admitted, even by Haeckel, as we have seen, that it has not been shown that living plants or animals ever did arise from not-living matter. But while admitting this he declares that "spontaneous generation" is not *impossible*, and that "a

GOD REIGNS 55

truly natural and consistent view of organisms can assume no supernatural act of creation.— [History of Creation, Volume I, page 48.] But living organisms exist; they must have arisen, according to Haeckel's own views, from the not-living, and in violation of all known natural laws—as clearly a miracle as any recorded in the New Testament. Tyndall, we have seen, admits that "it is no departure from scientific method to place behind natural phenomena a universal Father, who * * * alters the current of those phenomena—within certain limits—as he says in the same paragraph. Does the calling into life of the not-living exceed those limits, and must *that* event occur only under the agency of natural laws?

Then it would appear that nature may work a miracle when God may not.

But it is not here assumed that the coming of living creatures into being is any more miraculous than is the upholding of that being and controlling all subsequent changes, by evolution, or otherwise. God is in all and over all. And while, probably, there was neither plan nor design *in the human sense* in the calling of living creatures into being, there was that divine purpose and adaptation which needed not consideration, or reasoning, or any manner of ratiocination, which is in harmony with infinite intelligence, knowing all things from the beginning. When we go down, mentally, to the base of the series of fossiliferous rocks, and trace the history of living forms in the waters, advancing from age to age in constantly improving series of higher and more complex forms, we reach a period when to allow progress in new directions it became necessary to strain the excess of carbonic acid from the atmosphere and prepare it for the use of air-breathing animals. The admission of this fact and the process by which relief came is common among geologists and evolutionists. All plants and all forms of animal life were inhabitants of the waters. The atmosphere was surcharged with carbonic acid to such a degree that few plants and no animals respiring by lungs could exist in it. Should it remain thus all orders of life above algæ among plants and fishes among animals would continue apparently forever impossible. Then what happened was this: New forms of vegetation spread themselves over the saline marshes and low lands, over a large part of the earth, and for ages decomposed the carbonic acid in the air, leaving the oxygen free, and storing away the solid carbon in their own structures by the respiratory action of their foliage and green surfaces; and these carboniferous masses became fossilized and were stored away in the coal beds of the carboniferous period. More highly organized plants successively followed; and certain frogs, newts and a few insects became the forerunners of the more perfect races which were to breathe the purified air after the coal plants had done their preparatory work.

Was this great change brought about simply by the mechanical process of Natural Selection and adaptation and the law of inheritance? Haeckel answers in the affirmative: "Now, if we look back upon the whole history of the development of the vegetable kingdom, we cannot but perceive in it," he declares "a grand confirmation of the Theory of Descent. The two great principles of organic development which have been pointed out as the necessary results of natural selection in the struggle for life, namely: the laws of *differentiation* and *perfecting*, manifest themselves everywhere in the development of the larger and smaller groups of the natural system of plants. In each larger or smaller period of the organic history of the earth, the vegetable kingdom increases both in *variety* and *perfection*. During the whole of the long primordeal period there existed only the lowest and most imperfect group, that of the Algæ. To these are added, in the primary period, the higher and more perfect Cryptogamia, especially the main class of Ferns. During the coal period the Phanerogamia begin to develop out of the latter," etc. " Thus," he concludes, " in each succeeding later division of the organic history of the earth the vegetable kingdom gradually rose to a higher degree of perfection and variety." [History of Creation, Volume L, page 115.]

Here Haeckel appeals to a law of "perfecting" as aiding in all these changes. In the proper place we shall inquire further into this "higher law" of *perfecting:* it is sufficient here to allude to the fact that Haeckel finds it necessary to appeal to this *internal* agent in controling the variability of organisms. And he and other evolutionists, constantly refer to this *internal* element in the modification of organisms. It no doubt exists. But it did *not* exist in the few original specks of dead protoplasm before they were made alive; how then, did *these* determine their own, or the organization of their offspring? They could not transmit that which they had not.

But turning more directly again to the purification of the air during the coal period :

When we remember that the whole course of nature was changed by this carbonic purification; that no creature living in the waters could inhabit this new world of dry land without dispensing with gills and growing a pair of lungs, changing his fins to paddles, or wings, or legs, and re-adjusting his whole organism to a new life, it may be suspected (by those who deny the presence of God in all things), that here is a case where Tyndall should admit that "a heavenly Father behind natural phenomena" had, in a certain degree, changed the order of the phenomena. For certainly it is beyond the mechanical agency of the "struggle for existence," the survival of the fittest, organic adaptability and transmission by inheritance to offspring, to have worked up such a disposition to leave the waters for the dry land, and to devise or achieve the decarbonization of the air. Having now considered the agency of plants in preparing the earth's surface for the habitation of more perfect plants and of air-breathing animals, we turn to consider the mechanical laws of evolution (as they are termed), and see if they also do not require the intelligent volition of God in whom we live, and move and have our being.

And first, as to that important element in evolution which Darwin calls the struggle for existence, and that internal power of adaptability by which organisms conform themselves to the changes in their environments, and so survive their competitors in the struggle who are less able to conform themselves to changed conditions, and thus effecting a natural selection of improved forms and functions. Of this Mr. Darwin says: "It may metaphorically be said that Natural Selection is daily scrutinizing throughout the world the slightest variations; rejecting those that are bad, preserving and adding all that are good; silently and insensibly working whenever and wherever opportunity offers, at the improvement of each organic being in relation to organic and inorganic conditions of life." [Origin of Species, 5th edition, page 96.]

Attention is called to the declaration in these eloquent lines that "nature" is constantly striving for betterment. Other evolutionists teach the same; all work together for advancement, improvement, a higher good. From which it appears, according to the admission of evolutionists, that nature—or natural laws—or at least the course of evolution, tends toward and results in a progressive improvement, greater excellence and higher character, in a manner so closely resembling what should occur under the beneficent intelligence of divine power as to make it most reasonable to conclude that indeed God directed the waters "to bring forth abundantly the moving creature that hath life." The whole course of creation and evolution has proceeded *as if* controlled by intelligent volition, though there may have been neither constructive design nor anything in the nature of *human reason* in the adaptation which has certainly been constantly manifested. "God's thoughts are not as our thoughts;" and His infinite Order and eternal now direct the volitions which belong to himself, and not to the obedient atoms which forever work His will. Even Haeckel admits a qualified idea of God—"the sublime idea of the unity of God and nature." But it is noticeable that he assigns no part in the creation to God, but gives to "nature" all the glory.

Next in the scheme of evolution, and equal in importance with variability in conformity with the environment and survival of the fittest, is heredity, or "the laws of Transmission by Inheritance." The idea involved in the word heredity also underlies the phrase applied by Moses to plants and animals: "Let the earth bring forth grass, the herb yielding seed and the fruit-tree yielding fruit *after his kind.*" * * * "And let the earth bring forth the living creature *after his kind.*" It is that physiological law by which an acorn—the seed of an oak—always produces an oak, and not an apple tree; and by which the offspring of a rat is always a rat, and not a rein-deer, or some other animal. And one of the chief issues between evolutionists and others is as to whether these transmissions are limited by definite bounds which are never passed, or unlimited, so that all forms of organisms have come by evolution out of a few primary and very simple ones. We have seen that Haeckel maintains the latter view and declares that all forms have come by "natural selection," "working without a purpose." And he refers to what are known as "rudimentary organs—those exceedingly remarkable structures in plants and animals which have no object, and which he declares refute every teleological explanation seeking the final purpose of the organism [History of Creation, Volume I, page 26]; but which, on the contrary, appear to demonstrate that very purpose which he denies. For, when an organ no longer used shrinks away and becomes rudimentary, the *purpose* for which it had existed having failed, it would be charging God with folly did it fail to shrink away. When the muscles which once moved the human ear are no longer needed and are not used, they ought to shrink away; they no longer serve a purpose. When the eyes of fishes in the darkness of some cavern have remained useless and unused for many generations, they no longer serve a purpose, and ought to disappear as they do.

In further exclusion of God from all complicity in the evolution of living forms by adaptation and heredity, Haeckel declares that "where teleological dualism seeks the thoughts of a capricious creator in the miracles of creation, causal monism finds in the process of development the necessary effects of *eternal, immutable laws of nature.*" [History of Creation, Volume I, page 34.]

But laws are of themselves nothing but the statement of the usual modes of action. And if it is meant that these "eternal and immutable laws" are active forces, compelling results, then the *laws* are endowed with all the attributes of God, and compel that wise adaptation which is in accordance with the highest purpose. And as they act harmoniously and in unison throughout the universe, there should be no objection to the acceptance of Tyndall's suggestion, and the placing of God behind (or within and over) the phenomena.

One more declaration of Haeckel, in opposition to beneficence in nature and against the existence of God, and we leave direct consideration of the subject of evolution. Haeckel says: "If we contemplate the common life and the mental relations between plants and animals (man included), we shall find everywhere and at all times, the very opposite of that kindly and peaceful social life which the goodness of the Creator ought to have prepared for his creatures—we shall find everywhere a pitiless, most embittered struggle of *all against all*. Nowhere in nature, no matter where we turn our eyes, does that idylic peace, celebrated by the poets, exist; we find everywhere a struggle and a striving to annihilate neighbors and competitors. Passion and selfishness—conscious or unconscious—is everywhere the motive of life." [History of Creation, Volume 1, page 19.]

Is it indeed so? On the contrary, a more careful examination will show that this very struggle for existence is the proximate source of all the pleasures of living. It must be remembered, as taught by Haeckel and all evolutionists, that the races of plants and animals, in past and present time, are *one*, connected in a living and unbroken series from their earliest progenitors, so that the present races are but projections of the past by unbroken filiation, dying at one extremity and living at the other. When we consider this, then it will be seen that death, the fall of the unfittest in the competition for subsistence, and the evolution of higher and more complex forms of life, bring with them constantly widening pleasure and prosperity for the living. The preceding forms constantly disappear, like unused parts, become superfluous, and for the same reason, and are followed by a constantly rising and still perfecting progeny. Not only so, but as death and life are necessarily concomitant, the extinction of the falling individuals ministers to the welfare of the survivors. But not only are the races the gainers by this exterminative struggle, but individuals also; for by a beneficient provision in the condition of all organisms, their highest pleasure comes from the exercise and use of their faculties. There is no pleasure, no happiness, without this *use* of the faculties; and in the less elevated forms of sentient organisms, the competition, the exertion in search of subsistence, the necessary effort to maintain existence, and even the struggle which ends in death and the extinction of the weaker, ministers to the pleasure of the survivors; while the suffering of the defeated is comparatively brief and only the hastening of that death which is under all conditions inevitable. And if, as has been said, "there is nothing of which nature is so prodigal as life," so also is there nothing which she scatters abroad with so lavish and generous a hand. In the more advanced orders, and especially among mankind, the great and unending struggle has wrought out a code of ethics and made it inherent in the organism, in which love, and justice, and righteousness find their happiest manifestation, and toward which the race of mankind is advancing under that struggle which Haeckel declares to be "everywhere a pitiless, most embittered *struggle of all against all*," and are beginning to "beat their swords into ploughshares and their spears into pruning-hooks."

SERMON V.

"The Lord is good to all; and his tender mercies are over all his works."—Psalms, CXLV, 9.

It has been pointed out in previous discourses that teachers of science—both those who acknowledge God and those who do not —declare that there is in nature a constant progress toward improvement, and a better condition of both plants and animals—most summarily expressed in the words of Matthew Arnold, that there prevails "a power that makes for righteousness." Let us see if it may not as truly be said that *there is a power that makes for happiness.*

In the ninth chapter of "The Data of Ethics," Mr. Spencer has illustrated the fact that in the life of all organisms pleasure and the *use* or exercise of the faculties have from the first been evolved together. The extract is not a brief one, but should be given entire:

"During evolution there has been a superposing of the pleasures accompanying the uses of these successive sets of means; with the result that each of these pleasures has itself eventually become an end. We begin with a simple animal which, without ancillary appliances, swallows such food as accident brings in its way; and so, as we may assume, stills some kind of craving. Here we have the primary end of nutritition with its accompanying satisfaction, in their simple form. We pass to higher types having jaws for seizing and biting—jaws which thus, by their actions, facilitate achievement of the primary end. On observing animals furnished with these organs, we get evidence that the use of them becomes in itself pleasurable irrespective of the end : instance a squirrel, which, apart from food to be so obtained, delights in nibbling everything it gets hold of. Turning from jaws to limbs we see that these, serving some creatures for pursuit and others for escape, similarly yield gratification by their exercise; as in lambs, which skip, and horses which prance. How the combined use of limbs and jaws, originally subserving the satisfaction of appetite, grows to be in itself pleasurable, is daily illustrated in the playing of dogs. For that throwing down and worrying which, when prey is caught, precedes eating, is, in their mimic fights, carried by each as far as he dares. Coming to means still more remote from the end, namely, those by which creatures chased are caught, we are again shown by dogs that when no creature is caught there is still a gratification in the act of catching. The eagerness with which a dog runs after stones, or dances and barks in anticipation of jumping into the water after a stick, proves that apart from the satisfaction of appetite, and apart even from the satisfaction of killing prey, there is a satisfaction in the successful pursuit of a moving object. Throughout, then, we see that the pleasure attending on the use of means to achieve an end, itself becomes an end."

Now why should the coming of additional organs and functions, with the accompanying appetency for their exercise, invariably include a superadded pleasure? To insure the taking of food for the sustenance of the animal, appetite—hunger—appears to be of itself wholly sufficient. All the functions of the animal economy which are in any way under the control of volition involve an impulse, a disposition, a desire toward the use of the organs upon which they depend, which appears to be not at all dependent upon the accompanying pleasure or satisfaction. And the law of exercise or use of each organ or faculty, is, that while that is insured by an impulse or desire, the action itself is pleasurable. Is not that a beneficent law? And is that which is called Nature (apart from God) beneficent? Does that comprehensive doctrine of the Correlation of Forces include *love* as one of its correlates? Then indeed must we refer all modes of force and all expressions of energy back to God, "whose tender mercies are over all his works;" for it would appear that no mind which has not been debauched by a vain philosophy, can conceive of gravitation, or any correlated mode of *pressure or traction*, filling a world with gratuitous loving-kindness.

When we rise above the races nearest to man in multiplicity of functions and their concomitant pleasures, and consider man himself, we find that in him not only are those social affections common to both, more useful in character and more loaded with gratuitous pleasures, but we find also that many functions which are comparatively rudimentary in animals have been so exalted in man as to but little resemble those out of which, we are taught, they have arisen. And moreover, man possesses functions which are scarcely if at all to be found in the lower animals. Let us consider some of these—using for definitions the names suggested by Dr. Spurzheim:

1. The Reflecting Faculties, Comparison and Causality, which manifest the function of reason or ratiocination—the first determining *relations*, and the second considering their *dependencies*. What a wonderful system of co-ordinated organs and faculties minister to these reasoning powers! Senses that bring them reports from without, and perceptions which compound these into the data of reasoning within. Eyes that over and above the perception of light and shade, which alone appears sufficient for the vision of form and movement, but which have super-added notations of color, full of delights; ears which not only have the sense of sound, but bring

us "the sweet music of speech" and all the harmonies of string and reed, and organ-pipe —exquisite gifts of Beneficence not at all needful to the acutest hearing; taste, that charms the tongue and palate with countless sweets—superfluous, but for the free gift of loving kindness, where appetite and hunger alone were sufficient; and all the unnamed delights of the other senses, manifestly not essential to their specific functions: all these reporting the outer world to the inner faculties of perception, then on to the reflecting faculties for ratiocination.

And as to the Reflecting faculties themselves: it might be conceded that in their special function there is no proof of love in their office; for if man is to dominate all animals, to inhabit all climes, to fit himself to all environments, to guide and determine his own evolution and elevation, and compel the powers of nature to do his will, he must possess very high abilities as a reasoner. But a divine love has lighted the pathway where his reason moves; the very act of reasoning is full of gratification; and in its exercise man has subdued the earth to his use; he has organized the production and distribution of food and raiment, fenced out the storms of winter, filled his habitation with artificial warmth and compelled the elements to minister to his happiness. Prof. Haeckel thinks all these things are the result of mechanical evolution, not only without beneficent design, but without any intelligent purpose whatever. We prefer to look upon them and to receive them as the results of a kind Father's loving kindness, wrought out by his own laws of evolution.

2. But higher, more noble and more Godlike than the reasoning faculties is Benevolence—the sentiment which gives us happiness in making others happy. It is not necessary to debate the question as to whether this impulse of benevolence is wholly unselfish. Its exercise gives to him who feels it the most exalted happiness, and is, no doubt, so far selfish; but its specific object is the welfare of others; and the enjoyment which accompanies the manifestation of love toward others is superadded, and not needful to the end, which is the welfare of others; for an impulse wholly void of gratification in the benevolent would suffice. It is only within com-

paratively recent times, and in the most highly developed nations that this sentiment of Benevolence has become a dominating trait ; and in the history of the race but One alone has reached complete fullness in the sentiment and practice of unselfish and unconditional love toward all men: Jesus, the Nazarene. But his spirit, his teachings and his deeds now animate thousands, among *"believers"* and among unbelievers in the Christian church. And Shakespeare in his day knew the re-acting power of love and mercy, which come back in compound interest to the merciful. He makes Portia say to shylock :

"The quality of mercy is not strained ;
It droppeth as the gentle rain from heaven
Upon the place beneath ; it is twice bless'd ;
It blesseth him who gives and him who takes."

And it is so with every act of unconditional benevolence ; it blesses him that gives and him that takes. If material atoms organized by unconscious natural laws may evolve such results as these, then are material atoms and natural laws most God-like : let us rise above these to God himself.

3. Conscientiousness : The feeling of *right*

and *wrong ;* of *duty ;* of *ought* and *ought not* ; which when disobeyed and outraged induces a sense of guilt, and when obeyed is accompanied with satisfaction in a degree co-equal with the sacrifice involved. This sentiment is not the same as that last considered. Many persons possess it in a high degree who have little benevolent feeling ; and the existence of a strong emotion of unselfish love toward others with at the same time a dull sense of justice is a remarkable feature of the present age. Large numbers of dishonest people are found who have little or no sense of guiltiness for wrong, and yet whose outflowing benevolence is a leading motive of character. And on the other hand, there are many of those whose exact justice is unquestionable, but to whom the sentiment of disinterested benevolence and acts of spontaneous kindness are strangers.

The beneficent effect of justice toward others requires no proof ; but that this disposition is not a mere social impulse for the good of the race by action towards others, but is accompanied with a profound satisfaction in the exercise of the conscientious sentiment, indicates beneficent purpose or end, in the origin of the emotion.

The prophet Micah appears to have had a clear view of the distinction between this emotion of justice and that of benevolence, when he inquires: "What doth thy God require of thee but to do justly, and to love mercy, and to walk humbly with thy God." [Micah VI, 8].

4. Marvelousness: Wonder — Faith — Spirituality—Superstition; the sentiment is known by all these names. Its specific function is difficult to determine; but it has shown itself among all peoples and in all ages. It is not only unreasoning, but it is scarcely at all under the control of reason when manifested in fetichism, sorcery, charms, ghosts and a hundred forms of superstition among the ignorant. It gives the feeling of the supernatural; and it persists as some such feeling against all reason among many otherwise intelligent people. In its higher development it appears as the feeling of superstition, or of unreasonable faith as distinguished from intelligent belief and trust, based upon the intuition of the unseen. And joined with the

next sentiment to be considered—veneration—is the basis of the God-sentiment, which in some form or degree is found among all peoples. Paul, in his address to the Athenians, says: "Ye men of Athens, I perceive that in all things ye are too superstitious" [or *somewhat superstitious* or *religious*, in the margin.] for as I passed by and beheld your devotions, I found an altar with this inscription: 'To the unknown God!' Whom, therefore, ye ignorantly worship, him declare I unto you." [Acts, XXII, 23—*Revised version*].

And the apostle said this as if fully aware that the basal element of superstition and of enlightened faith is the same. At any rate, there can be no doubt of the widespread existence of this feeling, call it what we may. Now *what is it?* Can mechanical evolution have elevated a sentiment which relates to nothing? Hardly. And as this profound and inextinguishable feeling leads always to some form or degree of theism, reasonable men will "seek the Lord, if haply they might feel after him, though he be not far from every one of us."

5. Veneration: This is the last of the

sentiments named by Dr. Spurzheim demanding special attention in the scheme of these discourses. Literally, it is the sentiment or emotion of worship, and being blind—having in itself no element of knowledge—its manifestation and direction have always been and must be, according to the intelligence of the worshipper, base and cruel and groundless superstition in one, and the reverent uplifting of thankful devotion toward all-loving God in another.

Leaving all attempt to prove the existence of this sentiment, which is and has always been as common to mankind as hunger or thirst, there remains the question: Is its growth among men beneficent? It has been evolved and perfected under the same law of betterment with all other functions, and appears to relate properly only to that Infinite Love and Wisdom which has ever been the thread of unity, power and beneficent progress, and under whose control "all things make for righteousness." Whether its development in its highest estate is an individual *good* depends upon the individual; just as in music, poetry, art, and the entire sum of the æsthetic, the good is as the individual who is able to receive it. "And they are elevated in the scale of manhood, humanity, and all that is virtuous and ennobling, in proportion as they approach the worship of the God of Love," and imitate his never failing loving kindness.

SERMON VI.

"And we know that all things work together for good to them that love God."—Romans, VIII, 28.

In whatever restricted sense Paul may have used the words which indicate the theme of this discourse, they are no doubt true in the broadest sense. But to love God in the broadest sense is to love his creatures, and especially to love our fellow men. And our relation to them and other sentient beings, and to the whole realm of nature, is such that our own welfare depends upon conformity with and obedience to all physical, physiological, social and moral laws affecting us. Strictly, then, to love God is to seek conformity with his will, whereby "all things work together for good." And it is interesting to find that *good*, for which all things work together, is so related to the love of others— men and animals—as to be the basis of morality, not only in the purest religious systems and in the experience of mankind, but in that scientific system so carefully deduced by Mr. Herbert Spencer from the history of mankind under the influence of evolution. In the third chapter of "The Data of Ethics," after examining the relation of special virtues to human happiness, he says: "Unless it is asserted that courage and chastity could still be thought of as virtues though thus productive of misery, it must be admitted that the conception of virtue cannot be separated from the conception of happiness-producing conduct; and that as this holds of all the virtues, however otherwise unlike, it is from their conduciveness to happiness that they come to be classed as virtues." And he concludes the chapter with these words: "So that no school can avoid taking for the ultimate moral aim a desirable state of feeling called by whatever name—gratification, enjoyment, happiness. Pleasure somewhere, at some time, to some being or beings, is an inexpungable element of the conception. It is as much a necessary form of moral intuition as space is a necessary form of intellectual intuition."

This treatise upon the data of ethics as they

have been unfolded in the history of the race has been seriously considered by many persons as dangerous to established doctrines of virtue. But Mr. Spencer expressly declares at the close of his second chapter, after stating the implications which he finds in evolution : " These implications of the Evolution Hypothesis, we shall now see harmonize with the leading moral ideas men have otherwise reached."

The religious doctrines taught by Paul, the experience of mankind and the deductions of science, then, all agree that to the loving and the obedient all things work together for good. It should follow that he who is best — most loving and most obedient to duty, all things considered—is happiest. And it appears to have been in this sense that Paul spoke when he declared that the good which results from the working together of all things should come to "them who love God;" for although a Jew, brought up at the feet of Gamaliel, under the Mosaic system which demanded obedience and the love of God as the sole end, and not for the sake of the loving and the obedient, Paul in his discourse to the Athenians says: "God that made the world and all things therein, seeing that he is Lord of heaven and earth, dwelleth not in temples made with hands; neither is worshipped with men's hands, *as though he needed anything*, seeing he giveth to all life, and breath, and all things." [Acts, XVII, 24, 25].

We are then to consider the love toward God as being love toward his sentient creatures and obedient conformity to his laws.

No one who comprehends this law of love and has its spirit wrought into his emotional nature will " needlessly set foot upon a worm." For, if "not a sparrow shall fall on the ground without your Father," as Jesus told his followers, " who giveth food to the young ravens when they cry," so should every sentient creature within our reach have the good will of men, consistently with their own welfare. The earth is not (as held by many) for man alone; but for every creature in his order. For long ages the vegetable kingdom and the lowest forms of animated beings possessed the earth, and only very slowly and gradually gave place to higher organisms capable of enjoying more. In that struggle for existence which we are assured has been and still is the law which brings the betterment of animals and men, mankind are entitled, equally with the beasts, to the benefit of the law, each in proportion to his fitness; and man may therefore subdue or exterminate his noxious inferiors, as these do their's; but the higher development of his intellectual and moral powers demands that man should extend his kindly feeling to all his inferiors, as well as toward his fellow men.

"But why should a noisome toad have been created?" inquires one; "why should rats or lizards or serpents exist?" asks another; the answer is—that they may enjoy their lives. If they enter into the great struggle with man, they must perish; but their wanton destruction is cruel. And among higher animals "a righteous man regardeth the life of his beast," and—

> "He prayeth best who loveth best
> All things both great and small;
> For the dear God who loveth us,
> He made and loveth all."

And that love has been so inwrought with our

own moral nature that its exercise results in a consequent good to ourselves. And here arises an important question : Are we to be guided in the exercise of conscientiousness and benevolence alone by the promptings of the emotions ? or should these unreasoning sentiments of justice and love be put under rule, like other emotions?

Treating of benevolence in a preceding discourse, it was pointed out that this was blind, like all emotions, and demanded the guidance of the reasoning powers. It follows that as men differ widely in that regard, and as even very intelligent reasoners have differed among themselves as to what are the just promptings of reason concerning the ethical conduct demanded of us, we should, if possible, have a moral code to which the intelligent and the good have joined in their approval. And while no one's conscience can be justly held to ethical rules made by others, in the manifestation of his moral attributes, yet his *acts* as towards others may, no doubt, be required to harmonize with the consentaneous judgment and experience of mankind, whenever he comes into practical relations with them.

Such codes, written or unwritten, appear to have existed among people well advanced in civilization in all ages. And it is worthy of remark that the code promulgated to the Jews near three thousand and four hundred years ago by their great law-giver, Moses, is to this day the basis of, and almost identical with, that now in vogue among the most enlightened and humane nations everywhere. That code has had the test of very long experience; and omitting such portions as were special to the Jews, must ever remain the standard, because it *harmonizes with the constitution of man.*

It will be noted also that in the Commandments as given by Moses, no appeal is made to the higher nature of men, for very few in that day were in such a condition of enlightenment as to be able to respond to such an appeal; and Moses wisely appeals only to the hope of reward and the fear of punishment: "visiting the iniquities of the fathers upon the children unto the third and fourth generation," and "showing mercy unto thousands" of them that keep the Commandments. Did Moses understand the law of heredity? He evidently knew many things which are not commonly set down to his intelligence. He evidently knew the necessity of rest for man and beast; and in commanding Sabbath observance, after including therein the son, the daughter, the man-servant, the maid-servant, the ox, the ass and the stranger within the gates, he adds: "That the man-servant and the maid-servant may rest as well as thou, and remember that thou wast a servant in the land of Egypt." [Deut. ix, 6.] Even the Mosaic Sabbath, then (as was said by Jesus afterward), "was made for man, and not man for the Sabbath."

The more the teachings of the Jewish lawgiver are examined in connection with the condition of his people, so recently "come out of bondage" with no settled belief on theistical or ethical subjects, and full of idolatrous prejudice, the clearer it will be seen that in teaching them monotheism to drive out their degrading idolatries, he was compelled to sanction the anthropomorphizing of God, and to permit them to conceive of a being of bodily shape with like passions as themselves; for they could conceive of no other. Let us be worthy of an age in which, instead of worshipping a man-like God, we are permitted to approach more and more toward the character of God-like men: we may advance in love toward our fellow men; and God is Love.

May there not be still another side to the statement that "all things work together for good to them who love God;" that conform to his laws. Do they work together for evil to them who violate the law of their being—that is, who do not love God? The constitution of man and his relation to the laws which control his existence compel an answer in the affirmative; and the Mosaic requirement of "Obey and live" is only the absolute expression of this truth; for it is only by conforming to the harmonious relation between our own constitution and those natural laws to which we are subject that good to ourselves and others is to be secured. But there is a widespread belief, even among intelligent persons, that the natural laws are sometimes constrained by divine power to work together *out of their accustomed order* for the good of the obedient and for punishment of the disobedient. But Paul does not promise that all things shall be *controlled* together for good by an interference in behalf of them who love God; the statement of Paul implies that in accordance with the usual and unvarying order of events, all things do so work together for good. Nor will obedience to some ot the laws of our being and a neglect to obey others secure the promised good. Jesus said to the people assembled on the mount: "Not every one that saith 'Lord, Lord,' shall enter into the kingdom of heaven, but him that doeth the will of my Father." At another time he said: "Woe unto you Scribes and Pharisees, hypocrites; for ye pay tithes of mint and anise and cummin, and have omitted the weightier matters of the law, judgment, mercy and faith."

But if no natural law (which is God's law) is ever distorted from its usual course that it may work together with all things for the good of the obedient, neither is the law turned aside for the punishment of evil-doers. The divine attributes considered in the first of this series of discourses clearly indicate that God can never find it necessary to violate his own laws; for knowing all things from the beginning, being immanent in all phenomena, and controlling harmoniously all things by the counsel of His will, a change of purpose or the suspension or turning aside of any of his laws is inconceivable. There can be no "special providence," for the divine government is at all times both special and general, with no variableness, "neither shadow of turning."

Summarizing what has gone before in this discourse, we have the following propositions —

1. They "who love God," and for whom it is said all things work together for good, are those who manifest godliness—God-likeness, in that they obey His laws and love His creatures.

2. The working together of all things is not altered in behalf of such as are to receive the good, but these must harmoniously work together with all things.

3. Neither is there any change for the punishment of the unloving and disobedient; who miss the good from failure to conform to its conditions.

These conclusions harmonize with that loving consciousness defined in the first of these discourses as God; with the experience of mankind in all ages; and with that far-reaching doctrine of science termed Evolution, many of whose disciples were at first so blinded by the light of the new revelation as to believe that at last a way was found by which the universe and all its phenomena may exist without God. But the reaction has begun. Already many are wavering, and one who stands among the highest declares that "it is no departure from scientific method to place behind natural phenomena a universal Father." Had he said *amid, in* and *through* all phenomena, the conception would have been complete. For the universe is not an infinite machine, wound up to run forever, but an orderly government under the reign of conscious power, by which, in which and through which all things work together for good. There is no readjustment of parts, for all parts are always right; no re-arranged plans, for the end is known from the beginning; no cataclysms, for order reigns everywhere and at all times; no "special providences," for the providence of God is universal and not subject to exceptions; and no possible variableness nor shadow of turning at any time. For

God is self-existent, comprehending all existence; infinite as His universe and comprehending all its parts; without personal form to be conceived by finite minds, but having a personality in his intelligent volition and His Fatherly love; and of infinite order in the succession of all phenomena, which are but His manifest volitions.

Nor is it to be understood as here taught, that God is a mere all-pervading energy, like gravitation, working blindly in consecutive phenomena, without volition; but that He is a being comprehensive of all being, who "is before all things, and by him all things consist."

Blessed he who rests in confidence on this loving Father, and is able at all times to exclaim, as did Hagar in the wilderness: "Thou God seest me!"

SERMON VII.

"He hath showed thee, O man, what is good, and what doth the Lord require of thee, but to do justly, and to love mercy, and to walk humbly with thy God."—Micah vi, 8.

It is now proposed to consider in their order the three closely co-ordinated sentiments before noted as Conscientiousness, Benevolence and Veneration, concurrently with that of Marvelousness, in the latter of which has arisen the "intuition of divinity," called by Herbert Spencer "the ghost theory."

And first of Conscientiousness, from which come the sense of the obligation to be just, the feeling of rightness and the aversion to wrong conduct toward others. It rests on a reciprocity between parties, by which the act of one demands an equal return from the other, in which it is unlike Benevolence, which demands no return, though both are necessarily elements of social life.

Justice, the direct outcome of this sentiment, implying as it does an obligation and equivalent return, appears to be not at all predicable of any possible relation between God and man; as there can be no obligation upon the one side and no equivalent return on the other, seeing that God is Lord of heaven and earth, dwelleth not in temples made with hands; neither is worshipped with men's hands, as though he needed anything, seeing that he giveth to all life, and breath and all things."

There are reciprocal relations of love and worship between God and man; but these are not relations of justice, springing as they do, out of divine love toward man, and admitting no return for his loving-kindness but love toward our fellow men, and a loving reverence toward God, not for His demand, but for our happiness.

The statement that there can be no relations of justice between God and man is startling to many devout persons. But consider it. Justice is based upon equivalency. But, in words of the well known hymn,

"What shall I render to my God
For all His gifts to me?"

Nothing — absolutely nothing. What shall the rolling worlds which are everywhere careering through space render to the Law of Gravitation? Nothing but obedience. And obedience is the sole return that God's reasoning creatures can render for all his lovingkindness; and even this obedience results not in a re-payment to the Ruler on a basis of justice, but only in increase of happiness to the obedient.

Abraham, touching the destruction of Sodom, is represented as inquiring: "Shall not the Judge of all the earth do right?" And they who hold that there are relations of justice between God and man repeat the same inquiry to-day. Undoubtedly He will. But let us distinguish between justice and the doing of that which is right, when there are no mutual obligations. Abstract, absolute rightfulness exists with God alone. With man the right and the wrong are conditional; with God there can be no conditions. With him might and right are one. By these he overthrew Sodom and Gomorrah, and he has since overthrown numerous cities with earthquake and storm; He has swept from the ancient ocean the untold millions of dead which he fossilized in the now rocky sediment; and He is at this hour decimating the population of the earth in death, regardless of all distinction between the evil and the good. All this is right because God does it; and were our vision as broad as His and our knowledge infinite, we should see that it is also all right in itself.

This human sentiment of Conscientiousness, then, has regard only to the social relations of mankind. It is not necessary here to consider the wide extent of its influence, remembering, however, that it relates to all voluntary actions which can be *right* or *wrong*, and especially to reciprocal rights and duties.

Mr. Spencer in *The Data of Ethics* (quoting a former letter of his on the subject), gives us this account on the rise of the moral sentiments in the race: "I believe that the experiences of utility organized and consolidated through all past generations of the human race, have been producing corresponding nervous modifications which, by continued transmission and accumulation, have become in us certain faculties of moral intuition—certain emotions responding to right and wrong conduct, which have no apparent basis in the individual experiences of utility." There can, perhaps, be little doubt that this account of the rise of the moral sentiments is historically correct, for the savage and the barbarous races manifest them only in proportion to their elevation in the scale of civilization; that is, as man needed them more, they arose in his organization and became manifest in his moral nature. But it will be difficult for one who is untrammeled by a scientific regime to believe that this rise of the emotion of justice and right, and the conscientious repugnance to injustice and wrong, was the result solely of the necessities of men in their social relations, without the guiding control of the All-Good. Men without any active sense or emotion of justice may be forcibly compelled by their fellow men to act justly; but this compulsion does not awaken in the unwilling man an emotion of justice. And in the same manner men in society might have been—nay, must have been—compelled by their mutual relations, without the accompanying sentiment, or any awakening of a corresponding conscientious disposition to do right for its own sake.

This sentiment of conscientiousness is the basis of the most profound emotion of which man is capable. But like all modes of emotion it is blind; it does not know—it only feels; and hence it cannot alone give any rule of right or wrong. Under a blind impulse of duty unenlightened by the intellect, men have committed the most heinous deeds of wrong toward each other in the name of justice; and it is only after they have risen to a more elevated conception of God that they become aware that no relations of justice can exist with him. Ignorant of this, even Paul, subsequently the Christian apostle, declares that in zeal toward God he had persecuted Christians unto death.

The ruder races, and individuals in the most enlightened ones, imagine that God may be propitiated; that sacrifices are acceptable to him; that he demands a return for all blessings conferred, "as though he needed anything;" that they must do something for God, who has done so much for them. But Samuel, the prophet, said unto Saul: "Behold, to obey is better than sacrifice." And in Proverbs it is said; "To do justice and judgment is more acceptable to the Lord than sacrifice."

Conscientiousness, then, is an emotion which prompts to justice among men in society; to acts of righteousness and the avoidance of all that the enlightened intellect discovers to be wrong. It is therefore a principal element in the religious emotions, giving that controlling sense of duty which results in a happy satisfaction when obeyed, and in painful feelings of guilt and remorse when disobeyed.

Mr. Spencer, in reconciling conflicting ethical theories, says: "That happiness is the supreme end is beyond question true; for this is the concomitant of that higher life which every theory of moral guidance has distinctly or vaguely in view;" and he declares that the moral sentiments as guides "are proximately supreme solely because they lead to the ultimately supreme end, happiness, special and general." So that by the laws and progress of "Evolution" it is shown that the supreme end of life is the happiness of the living.

But Mr. Spencer is far from admitting (however he may believe), that a divine Will and an infinite Love so control the evolution of sentient creatures as to secure that supreme end. "If for the divine Will," he says, supposed to be supernaturally revealed, we substitute the naturally revealed end toward which the Power (the capital P is his) manifested throughout Evolution works; then, since Evolution has been and is still working toward the highest life, it follows that conforming to those principles by which the highest life is achieved, is furthering that end." [Data of Ethics, § 62.]

This appears to be an example in which the name of God is purposely avoided in alluding to the "Power through which Evolution works" in conformity with the established custom among certain teachers of science, of ignoring God. "The Power through which Evolution works" is God; and it required some ingenuity to speak of his controlling will without calling his name.

From what has been said, then (and in this agnostic scientists concur), the Sentiment of Conscientiousness relates wholly to men in their social state. It is only in conjoint action with Veneration that the feeling of duty toward God arises; but as even this sentiment of adoration, like all feelings, has the happiness of the worshipper as its end, its manifestation can have no obligatory relation toward God. He who never lifts his heart toward God in profound veneration is himself the only loser.

Mr. Spencer (and others less elaborately) has traced the rise and evolution of this preeminent emotion among men in society. Summing up his conclusions in the letter quoted above, and afterwards referring to this summary, he says: "Conscientiousness has in many out-grown that stage in which the sense of a compelling power is joined with rectitude of action. The truly honest man, here and there to be found, is not only without thought of legal, religious or social compulsion, when he discharges an equitable claim on him; but he is without thought of self-compulsion. He does the right thing with a simple feeling of satisfaction in doing it; and is, indeed, impatient if anything prevents him from having the satisfaction of doing it." [Data of Ethics, § 46.]

Now, all this relates to the sentiment of moral obligation. But Mr. Spencer also attempts to account for the rise and evolution of the happy satisfaction which accompanies the manifestation of the moral sentiment—as of all the feelings. His conclusion is: "Those races of beings only can have survived in which, on the average, agreeable or desired feelings went along with activities conducive to the maintenance of life, while disagreeable and habitually avoided feelings went along with activities directly or indirectly destructive of life; and there must ever have been, other things equal, the most numerous and long-continued survivals among races in which these adjustments of feelings to actions were the best, tending ever to bring about perfect adjustment." [Data of Ethics, § 33.] The manifest result of which is, that when life can no longer be enjoyed, it ceases. But why is satisfaction — pleasure — happiness the very *sine qua non* of life? And how does the consciousness of it "arise?" On this point Prof. Tyndall says in the Belfast address: "We can trace the development of a nervous system, and correlate with it the parallel phenomena of sensation and thought. We see with undoubting certainty that they go hand in hand. But we try to soar in a vacuum the moment we seek to comprehend the connection between them. * * * All that has been here said is to be taken in connection with this fundamental truth. When 'nascent senses' are spoken of, when the 'differentiation of a tissue at first vaguely sensitive all over' is spoken of, and when these processes are associated with 'the modification of an organism by its environment,' the same parallelism without contact is implied. There is no fusion possible between the two classes of facts—no motor energy in the intellect of man *to carry it without logical rupture from one to the other."* This is a most important and very candid statement ; and will again be referred to.

Herbert Spencer, touching the same matter, says : " Without questioning that the raw material of consciousness is present even in indifferentiated protoplasm, and everywhere exists potentially in that Unknowable Power which, otherwise conditioned, is manifested in physical action, I demur to the conclusion that it at first exists (in the simplest organisms) under the forms of pleasure and pain." [Note to § 33, Data of Ethics.]

The whole sentient world is constituted on

the necessity of happiness in some form or degree to the persistence of life ; and the only deference which Mr. Spencer — the most voluminous writer of the age—can find space to offer that "Unknowable Power" which ordains life and happiness together, is to refer to it in capital letters. The rise and essence of all degrees of feeling and of consciousness (except historically) are "unknowable" (as admitted by Tyndall); but writers (including Herbert Spencer) among the ablest scientists, do not on that account hesitate to treat at great length on the work of that unknowable power. Even Professor Haeckel admits the existence of an inscrutable "perfecting power" by which all living creatures are being "improved;" and Professor Tyndall, as has been shown, while declaring that "the whole process of evolution is the manifestation of a Power absolutely inscrutable," and that considered fundamentally, it is by the operation of an insoluable mystery that life is evolved, species differentiated and mind unfolded from their preponent elements in the immeasureable past," declares nevertheless that "prolonging the vision backward across the boundary of the experimental evidence," he discerns in matter "the promise and potency of every form and quality of life."

Now, in treating so widely and wisely of the "Power" which has controlled "the whole process of evolution," why do so many writers utterly ignore God? It would hardly be presumption if some devout Paul should say to them: "Him declare I unto you!" They consider the mysterious Ether, the existence of which is an unproved hypothesis, give it a name and laboriously trace its office in the universe. They build an entire system of philosophy upon Gravity, known to them solely by its effects. And yet, when speaking of the Infinite Unity by which all things exist, subsist and consist, they declare Him to be "unknowable," and decline to speak His name. Mr. Spencer goes so far as to say: "The Power which *the universe manifests to us* is utterly inscrutable" [First Principles, Chapter II, page 46]; and Tyndall, in similar phrase, says: "The whole process of evolution is the manifestation of a Power absolutely inscrutable to the intellect of man." [Belfast Address.] And a few lines further on he declares: "We have the conception that all we see around us and all we feel within us—the phenomena of physical nature as well as those of the human mind—have their inscrutable roots in a cosmical life, if I dare apply the term, an infinitesimal span of which only is offered to the investigation of Man." And in that investigation Mr. Tyndall himself labors with loving ardor. Very well. The power which we call Gravity is also utterly inscrutable, except as "the universe manifests to us" its existence by its effects. Are we to ignore that wide-reaching energy which operates without regard to time or space, because its nature is inscrutable and we are not yet able to determine whether all known modes of energy do not arise as its correlations? If not, then by far greater reason should we not pronounce as "unknowable" and refuse "to feel after" God, who "created the heavens and the earth."

A few considerations as to the importance of understanding that Conscientiousness is not an intellectual power, having the function of *knowing*, but only that of *feeling*, and this discourse will be ended.

It is but too well known that under opposing views of what was undoubtingly believed to be the teaching of conscience, the blood of opposing brethren has flowed in the conflict of "holy wars;" persecution for opinion's sake has planted the stake and fagot of superstition; and all manner of wrong and outrage have been justified by appeals to conscience, under its honest but ignorant promptings. The history of Conscience in the progress of the race has been a sad and a humiliating one. But on the other hand, as mankind have risen to the fundamental truth that Conscientiousness, great and momentous as is its true function, is only a feeling, and void of all capacity to *know*, and requiring the guidance of the intellect, even as the lowest propensities do, it has risen to the very first importance in the social relations of enlightened nations. And when acting conjointly with the group of the religious sentiments also fully enlightened, it promises to be a chief factor in the elevation of the race to its highest happiness.

Whether, as quoted from Mr. Spencer above, "Conscientiousness has in many (or any) outgrown that stage in which a compelling power is joined with rectitude of action," may be considered as very doubtful. The physiological law is, that all faculties and functions based in the nervous system, increase by use — by their proper exercise. It is therefore difficult to perceive how the feeling can become less by its appropriate exercise, even though its possessor "does the right thing with a simple feeling of satisfaction in doing it." But possibly the full meaning of this statement has not been apprehended, and has been sufficiently qualified by the accompanying statement "that with some of the fundamental other-regarding duties, the sense of obligation " *has retreated into the background of the mind*," instead of fading out as moral actions become more pleasant. It is not very safe to differ from Mr. Spencer, whose depth and breadth of treatment of all the questions he discusses is the sufficient apology for referring to him so often.

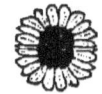

SERMON VIII.

" He that loveth not, knoweth not God ; for God is Love."—First Epistle of John IV, 8.

Benevolence—Good-will—is the Sentiment to be next considered.

In the present advanced condition of the race in civilized countries, it is, in its highest manifestation, an emotion not directly selfish, but is essentially a desire for the welfare of others. But though not in itself demanding or even expecting any return, as does the emotion of Conscientiousness, its action is in itself accompanied with pleasure, and often with the highest happiness.

Mr. Darwin, in *The Descent of Man*, has treated of this emotion together with the other moral sentiments, without discriminating with any care between them. He appears to think that the love of approbation was among the chief agencies in promoting its rise and evolution; but of the *origin* of the intellect (in which he appears to include the sentiments and feelings), he says: " In what manner the mental powers were first developed in the lowest organisms, is as hopeless an inquiry as how life first originated." [American Edition, page 35.]

As an instance of Mr. Darwin's want of discrimination between the different moral sentiments are these words on page 67 of above work: " I fully subscribe to the judgment of those writers who maintain that of all the differences between man and the lower animals, the moral sense or conscience is by far the most important. This sense, as Mr. McIntosh remarks, 'has a rightful supremacy over every other principle of human action;' it is summed up in that short but imperious word *ought*, so full of high significance. It is the most noble of all the attributes of man, leading him without a moment's hesitation to risk his life for that of a fellow creature." But it is quite certain that Love—Benevolence—does not act under any sense of duty, or because it ought to: it is spontaneous in the presence of an appropriate object, and even sometimes acts in opposition to the promptings of conscience. But let it be noted that Mr. Darwin clearly places the moral sentiments of man above his reason, in a comparison with brutes.

Mr. Spencer has also treated of the rise and evolution of Benevolence at length. But though he appears to discriminate between the emotions of Conscientiousness and Benevolence — between Duty and Love,— he has generally grouped them under the general name of moral sentiments, though in their essential characters they are evidently quite distinct, demanding separate consideration.

What is meant in this discourse, then, by Benevolence, is Love, that emotion so well portrayed by Paul to the Corinthians under the name of Charity, which in the New Version is rendered Love. Says the Apostle: " Love suffereth long and is kind; love envieth not; love vaunteth not itself, is not puffed up, doth not behave itself unseemly, seeketh not its own, is not provoked, taketh not account of evil, rejoiceth not in unrighteousness, but rejoiceth in the truth; beareth all things, believeth all things, endureth all things.   *   *   *   Now abideth faith, hope, love, these three ; and the greatest of these is love." [First Corinthians XIII, 4-7, 13.]

It will require but little close observation to find that it is necessary to discriminate between this sentiment and that which prompts to justice, equity, duty and all emotions which are accompanied with the feeling that we *ought* to manifest them. Indeed — in the United States at least — justice appears to be declining, while benevolence has increased beyond example. Large numbers of persons no way noted for justice, are so generous, so given to good-will toward others, as to be noted for their emotional love for their fellow men. Even the notably dishonest, the vile, the law-breaker void of any strong sense of duty, will often be found to be spontaneously generous, kind and loving. They may "steal from the rich and give to the poor;" they may acquire wealth by dishonest means, and expend it in profuse charities from no motives but benevolence and the love of approbation. The whole land is filled with organizations of men, and of women, and of men and women combined, whose sole business it is to seek out and to relieve the suffering and the needy. But a fair acquaintance with the members of these associations will not show them to be more just in their private relations than others. There has been no time in the history of civilization when governments, associations of citizens and private individuals were so active in relieving poverty, misfortune, sickness, famine, ignorance and all human ills, as now. If these do not readily present themselves, the prevailing feeling of benevolence prompts to systematic search for them. Even crime is hardly a barrier to the expression of this sentiment, and criminals are often unworthy recipients of spontaneous generosity from those who are not criminals.

On the other hand, honesty, especially in trade, is almost a forgotten virtue. Our tables are supplied with ground cocoanut shells for pepper, sulphuric acid for vinegar, corn-meal and curcuma for mustard, beans, chicory and other adulterations for coffee, sloe leaves for tea; and a hundred other similar frauds. For a quart of strawberries we get a pint, with all the large ones on top; other fruits are disguised by red gauze for the required ruddy hue, and blue gauze for grapes or plums which should look blue. Baking powders have alum for cream tartar, and horse-radish in bottles is half turnips, Candies are half *terra alba*, molasses half corn syrup and butter half lard. Even the medicines upon which life depends for genuineness, are often not only adulterated, but are often wholly factitious.

It will not be necessary to look at other departments of trade; they are nearly all much alike in this respect—only the counterfeit presentment of what honest trade should be. Nor is this want of honesty confined to tradesmen: it has found its way into nearly every rank and degree of society, from the boy who sells papers in the street upon a false cry of news to the minister who preaches another's sermon without giving just credit.

Now, nobody believes that all these people who manifest so little sense of justice and honesty are equally deficient in benevolence. Many of them are overflowing with "the milk of human kindness," and their hearts and their purses are open to all appeals for sympathy, and their hands ready for good deeds toward their fellow men.

But against all these, and further showing the essential difference between Conscientiousness and Benevolence, we shall find men who are in all things scrupulously honest, but whose generosity is never manifested; men who "do justly" and, apparently, "walk humbly before God," but who never give proofs that they also love mercy." They may be conscientious to a notable degree, but those who know them best, and admit this virtue, never ask their aid in any labor of love; never see their names on any list of kind-hearted citizens, acting for the relief of the suffering, and never complaining of their cold selfishness, saying: "They are honest, but they do nothing for charity's sake." Every observer must have known examples of this kind; and they generally everlook the heartlessness in deference to the honesty.

These considerations are enough to show that the Sentiments of Conscientiousness and Benevolence are not identical, and that the one may be strong and the other weak and rarely wakened in the same individual. Haeckel suggests—he does not advocate—that there is danger that the sentiment of benevolence may become too strong, and ought to be restrained; and that the feeble, the diseased, the blind, the insane, ought to be abandoned to their fate, instead of building asylums for them and caring for them, lest the advancement of the race be interfered with; and he cites the American Indians as examples of savage selfishness in the destruction of feeble or diseased children. And even Mr. Spencer (Data of Ethics, Am. Ed., page 189) says, in defence of similar but far less savage views: "Any arrangements which in a considerable degree prevent superiority from profiting by the rewards of superiority, or shield inferiority from the evils it entails—any arrangement which tends to make it as well to be inferior as to be superior, are arrangements diametrically opposed to the progress of organization and the reaching of a higher life." And he adds that "under its biological aspect this proposition cannot be contested by those who agree in the doctrine of Evolution; but probably they will not at once allow that the admission of it under its ethical aspect is equally unavoidable. While, as respects the development of life, the well-working of the universal principle described is sufficiently manifest, the well-working of it as respects the increase of happiness may not be seen at once. But the two cannot be disjoined."

The same author appears to doubt the disinterestedness of those who manifest apparently unselfish benevolence, and declares (p. 199) that "a society in which the most exalted principles of self-sacrifice for the benefit of neighbors are enunciated may be a society in which unscrupulous sacrifice of alien fellow-creatures is not only tolerant but applauded." If this refers to a State as a society, the statement may in many cases be true; because there are many classes in a State, and the public rulers are not always benevolent, while many of its citizens may be so; but it is hardly true that societies composed of private individuals united for professedly benevolent objects, can be justly charged with this gross inconsistency. And even were it otherwise, it does no more discredit to genuinely disinterested benevolence than do the offenses practiced by tradesmen to justice and righteousness.

In opposition to what appears to be the views of at least some of the Evolutionists, we shall hold that this God-like Sentiment of

Love can never become excessive; though being an unreasoning emotion, and not having any mode of knowledge as its function, it demands the controlling and directing supervision of the reasoning powers. But Benevolence in the highest sense and in all its variety of manifestations must become the ruling emotion among men, or they cannot maintain their claim of great superiority over the brutes. If the race dies of brotherly-love it will be a glorious consummation, and extinction will become the very acme of life.

In Christianity and in all the higher forms of religious expression, Benevolence plays a ruling part among the group of the religious sentiments; and it is that which has finally subdued superstition to so great an extent, acting under the guidance of a freer and more enlightened intellect.

Did this divine Sentiment exist as "the raw material" of Spencer, or as a "promise and potency" as an element of primeval matter where Professor Tyndall's backward vision discerned it? or does it come directly from the loving God who is immanent in all matter, unorganized as well as organized? Let each answer for himself, according as his love abounds; but, as we have seen, Mr. Darwin admits that the origin of the intellect and feelings "is an inquiry as hopeless as how life originated;" and no Evolutionist pretends to tell exactly how intellect and feeling first arose, though they treat with confidence of the causes and processes of their evolution. And according to Professor Tyndall, " it is no departure from scientific method to place behind natural phenomena a universal Father," though he denies that his existence has been proven.

The office of this sentiment of Benevolence, like the underlying tendency of Evolution, is the common good, toward which and for which all evolution has proceeded. And that life exists that the living may enjoy it, Benevolence is correlative with the very essence of organic evolution. That, and not reason is the mother of social life. Reason protects no offspring, constitutes no families, binds together no tribes, erects no social organism. It wipes away no tears, holds up no hands of the weak or helpless, sympathises with no sorrow. It is simply a cold adjustment of sequences and consequences, heartless and unfeeling. But " Love seeketh not its own," and "blessed are the merciful for they shall obtain mercy."

There is found in the legislation of all nations another proof (not yet considered) that Conscientiousness and Benevolence are different in their nature. We have laws demanding that men shall be honest ; that the debtor "shall pay the uttermost farthing ;" that the thief, the forger, the burglar, the counterfeiter, the contract breaker, and all violators of justice shall be punished ; but no law commands men to be generous, charitable, loving and forbearing ; legislators are well aware that love of the neighbor cannot be had by compulsion, and that the charity which suffereth long, and is kind, envieth not, seeketh not its own, beareth all things, hopeth all things, endureth all things, cannot come by legislation. And he who has the legal right to demand his pound of flesh, can have no lawful demand for a single throb of loving kindness.

It is true the law demands that we shall do no murder, and that we shall abstain from acts of violence and all injury to the person of another ; but it does not demand that this abstinence shall be accompanied with emotions of kindness; it does not require that we should love our neighbor, but only that we shall do him no personal injury.

It has been already indicated that the Sentiment of Benevolence is intimately connected with the end toward which organic evolution tends : the happiness of the living. It has been shown that Herbert Spencer and other Evolutionists admit that the end for which evolution works is happiness, pleasure, satisfaction, or some mode or degree of sentient gratification ; Sixty years ago, Spurzheim (in the philosophical part of his work upon the brain), and after him Mr. George Combe, showed that all the faculties of man—of the body and of the mind—specifically relate to other faculties, functions, offices or necessities of the organism, or to something in its environment, upon which its existence and welfare depend. The muscles relate to the parts which are to be moved; the bones to the parts to be supported; the heart, arteries and veins to the blood to be circulated ; the brain and nervous system to the various functions of voluntary motion, sensation, emotion, reason, etc.; while each separate and specific mental faculty has some correlative with which it is related: Conscientiousness relates to justice; Idealty to the beautiful; Hope to anticipated good; Acquisitiveness to property. And in all these relations the faculties and their correlatives affect each other by interaction proper to each. Now, it is evident that if happiness is the end toward which Evolution has worked and is still working, man must himself not only present no obstacle to, but must become helpful toward, his own happiness by ministering to the happiness of others, and herein may be seen that Divine Love which is not only immanent in and works out through Evolution as its aim and end, the welfare and happiness of all sentient creatures; but by the same law raises up in man an emotion of love toward his fellow which ministers to that beneficent end, and which at the same time is filled with happiness in its own manifestation. So that love is co-ordinated with the happiness of others, while that happiness is reflected back to the loving heart which has manifested it.

And it has come about that, as declared by

the Apostle John: "He that loveth not, knoweth not God;" for it is in the thread of evolving creation, with Love as its essence, and Happiness as its end, that the loving "Father" (whose existence Tyndall declares has not been proven) is seen and felt and known by His loving children.

SERMON IX.

"In thoughts from visions of the night, when deep sleep falleth on men, fear came upon me, and trembling. * * * Then a spirit passed before my face."—Job IV, 13-15.

That specific emotion which Dr. Spurzheim called Marvelousness has been treated of under other names by many writers, and by Mr. Spencer at great length. He calls it "The ghost theory." It is of this sentiment that J. Allanson Picton, in *The Essential Nature of Religion*, speaks in the following words: "Since mankind are so constituted that in one form or another this sense of an ultimate positive mystery is, whether perceived or not, mixed up in all their thoughts, while it occasionally shows itself with portentous energy; it is inevitable that attempts should be made to give practical expression to the feeling. And in such efforts we have the very first germs of religion." But this statement treats of the sentiment not in its earlier forms, but in that of advanced evolution. Mr. Spencer attempts to trace the feeling to its source, and has with much labor and ingenuity pointed out the supposed origin—or origins, for he cites many—of "the ghost theory." To avoid doing him injustice, it will be necessary to quote his views somewhat fully, which is done from an extended *note* appended to his *Essay on Animal Worship*. After explaining his concurrence in certain views of Professor Huxley—namely: "that the savage, conceiving a corpse to be deserted by the active personality who dwelt in it, conceiving this active personality to be still existing, and that his feelings and ideas concerning it form the basis of his superstition;" he adds: "Everywhere we find expressed or implied the belief that each person is double; and that when he dies his other self, whether remaining near at hand or gone far away may return, and continues capable of injuring his enemies and aiding his friends." Mr. Spencer appends the note referred to, in which he recognizes the fact that Mr. Huxley's views show "the ghost theory" in an advanced state, without indicating its origin; and then attempts to fill "this wide gap in the argument" by indicating some of the means by which the ghost theory arose, as follows:

1. It is not impossible that his shadow, following him everywhere, and moving as he moves, may have some small share in giving to the savage a vague idea of his duality.

2. A much more decided suggestion of the same kind is likely to result from the reflection of his face and figure in water, imitating him as it does in his form, colors, motions, grimaces. When we remember that not unfrequently a savage objects to have his portrait taken, because he thinks whoever carries away a representation of him carries away some part of his being, will see how probable it is that he thinks his double in the water is a reality in some way belonging to him.

3. Echoes must greatly tend to confirm the idea of dualty otherwise arrived at. Incapable as he is of understanding their natural origin, the primitive man necessarily ascribes them to living beings—beings who mock him and elude his search.

4. The suggestions resulting from these and other physical phenomena are, however,

secondary in importance. The root of this belief in another self lies in the experience of dreams. The distinction so easily made by us between our life in dreams and our real life, is one which the savage recognizes in but a vague way, and he cannot express even that distinction which he perceives. When he awakes, and to those who have seen him lying quietly asleep, describes where he has been and what he has done, his rude language fails to state the difference between seeing and dreaming that he saw, doing and dreaming that he did. From this inadequacy of his language it not only results that he cannot truly represent this difference to others, but also that he cannot truly represent it to himself. Hence, in the absence of an alternative interpretation, his belief, and that of those to whom he tells his adventures, is that his other self has been away and came back when he awoke. And this belief, which we find among various existing savage tribes, we equally find in the traditions of early civilized races.

5. The conception of another self capable of going away and returning, receives what to the savage must seem conclusive verifications

from the abnormal suspensions of consciousness, that occasionally occur in members of his tribe. One who has fainted and cannot be immediately brought back to himself (note the significance of our own phrases, returning to himself, etc.) as a sleeper can, shows him a state in which the other self has been away for a time beyond recall. Still more is this prolonged absence of the other self shown him in cases of apoplexy, catalepsy and other forms of suspended animation. Here for hours the other self persists in remaining away, and on returning refuses to say where he has been. Further verification is afforded by every epileptic subject, into whose body, during the absence of the other self, some enemy has entered, for how else does it happen that the other self on returning denies all knowledge of what his body has been doing? And this supposition that the body has "been possessed" by some other being is confirmed by the phenomena of somnambulism and insanity.

6. What, then, is the interpretation inevitably put upon death? The other self has habitually returned after sleep, which simu-

lates death. It has returned, too, after fainting, which simulates death much more. It has even returned after the rigid state of catalepsy, which simulates death very greatly. Will it not return also after this still more prolonged quiescence and rigidity? Clearly it is quite possible — quite probable even. The dead man's other self is gone away for a long time, but it still exists somewhere, far or near, and may at any moment come back to do all he said he would do."

This long quotation is interesting in several ways. It indicates by its language that according to the most eminent Evolutionists a belief in immortality arose very early among even the least advanced savages, and also that even so profound a philosopher as Spencer finds it difficult to give any special reason for its existence, but suggests several which he thinks have conspired to awaken that belief: 1, men's shadows; 2, their reflection in the water; 3, echoes; and 4, the most important of all, "the experience of dreams." But after stating all these Mr. Spencer adds—apparently feeling that more were needed—suspensions of consciousness from fainting, apoplexy, catalepsy, etc. These views are not cited for the purpose of opposing them; for at some period in man's history and by some means or agency, the idea of spiritual existence (including that of immortality) has risen, and has become the germ of all religions containing these elements. Mr. Spencer says [Data of Ethics, § 18] referring to a certain school of morals:

"It originates with the savage whose only restraint beyond fear of his fellowmen is fear of an ancestral spirit." And he and other Evolutionists consider this ghost theory as the germ of all religions. It is also admitted that a *feeling* is the basis of the *theory;* but no sufficient attempt appears to have been made toward a discrimination between the blind Sentiment which *feels* and the knowing Intellect which theorizes. Marvelousness is simply an emotion, and like Conscientiousness, Benevolence, Veneration and all special sentiments, *there must be a correlative to which it is specially related.* Now, what is it that awakened the "ghost theory" which is admittedly the germ of all religions? Is it the shadow cast by the sun, the face reflected in the water; echoes coming back from a hillside, or dreams which arise "in thoughts from visions of the night," as when a spirit passed before the face of Job? As the feeling of the marvelous, the mysterious, the ghostly, has not only been the the source of all superstition, but, as admitted by the Evolutionists, of the religions of all civilized peoples, it cannot be "a departure from scientific method" to assume that spiritual exisience and immortality are the true correlatives of this early-awakened and wide-spread emotion among men. Something real—not merely imaginary—relates to and is correlated with this Sentiment, which has had a wider influence both for evil and for good than any other. And if the views of Mr. Spencer and others as to the manner in which the ghost theory first arose and has since been evolved in the religions of the most advanced nations are the true ones, let it be remembered that justice and benevolence arose in a similar manner from lower and more savage sentiments. And as Paul said to the Galatians, "the law was our schoolmaster to bring us to Christ," so have been all forms of superstition, including worship of ancestors, our schoolmaster to bring us unto God. Consciousness of God appears to be the end to which this emotion of Marvelousness has been tending from its first rudiments among men, too little above brutes, to have any reasonable conception higher than that of some dread mystery, up to him who declared that God is Love.

But let us distinguish between the emotion and the various theories based upon it. Theories are matters of the intellect, and men naturally differ in their ghost theories as much as they differ as to the emotion which prompts to do justice or any other. The impulse to do justly, differing only in degree, is the same in all; but the determination of what is just under any given state of facts is a matter of reason, about which men have always differed. So there can be no such thing as *the* ghost theory, although as high an authority as Mr. Herbert Spencer alludes to it with the definite article. There are great numbers of ghost theories; even Mr. Spencer has one of his own, when he speaks of "the Power which the universe *manifests to us.*" Professor Tyndall had one when he saw by his backward vision in the original nebula "the promise and potency of every form and quality of life." Even in its lowest form of an unreasoning (and ineradicable) superstitious response to the mysterious, the marvelous and the unknown, it is common still among most intelligent people. Mr. Picton, in the essay already referred to, says: "If a man can really think that the glory of the universe is explicable on the hypothesis of little indestructible and eternally dancing points of matter, which have no deeper reality within or beyond them; then, certainly, religion is in that man an incongruity, but it does not follow that he will be wholly destitute of it. For I do not for a moment believe that any man *can* think any such unthinkable absurdity. He may think that he thinks it; but that is all. What he really means is that there is no further explanation *possible*, however much it may be needed; and therefore he calls his atoms the ultimate explanation of the world. But that does not hinder him from many a moment of reverie, in which he recognizes in the universe some nameless Unity that awes his spirit to a silent worship."

To this Sentiment of Marvelousness is very closely allied — especially among cultivated people — that of Veneration or Reverence, which in its highest expression becomes worship. On the hypothesis of Evolution, it probably arose out of the former; and both sentiments are elements in all advanced phases of religious emotion. Mr. Spencer supposes it to have taken the form at an early period of the worship of ancestors, among many if not all races. In his essay on *The Origin of Animal Worship* he says: "The rudimentary form of all religions is the propitiation of dead ancestors, who are supposed to be still existing and to be capable of working good or evil to their descendants." And in the same essay he says: "The desire to propitiate the other self of the dead ancestor displayed among savage tribes, dominantly manifested by the old historic races, by the Peruvians and Mexicans, by the Chinese at the present time, and to a considerable degree by ourselves (for what else is the wish to do that which a lately deceased parent was known to have desired?) has been the universal first form of religious belief; and from it have grown up the many divergent beliefs that have been referred to."

Now, although there is some dissent among teachers of science as to the rise and line of evolution of the religious sentiments, it is evident that among eminent Evolutionists it is held that the sentiment distinctively known as Marvelousness—however it arose—has been the basis of all forms of the "ghost theory," and that all more recent manifestations of religious feeling and modes of worship have grown out of these. We have seen that according to the views of Evolutionists as well as others before the rise of the new science, Marvelousness and Veneration must have their correlatives to which they bear special relation, beyond the shadows, echoes and dreams which may have first awakened them. And we have seen that the indications all point to the worship of one God as the end to which all evolution has been tending.

At this point it becomes necessary to make a distinction which is too frequently neglected; a distinction between religion and theology. Religion pertains to the emotions, which feel, but do not think; theology to the intellect, where all doctrines, religious as well as others, have their rise. Strictly, there can be but one religion; while there are theologies without number. Of course it is not denied that with cultivated people religion must necessarily go hand-in-hand with some form of doctrine — some theological beliefs—without which the blind religious emotions would be as aimless and void of useful results as would be the blind feeling which impels to justice, without intelligent guidance.

The common habit of confounding religion with theology makes it difficult to give any satisfactory definition of religion. A definition offered by Mr. Picton, in the essay before cited, is: "Following the suggestion of great teachers, but carefully avoiding the snare into which some have fallen, of confounding religion with philosophy on the one hand, or with morality, on the other, we may define religion as being· in its essential nature an endeavor after a practical expression of man's conscious relation to the Infinite. * * * All I ask is that the phrase, 'conscious relation to the Infinite,' may be accepted as including every stage in the development of this consciousness, just as the name of a plant includes the germinating blade as well as the fruit-bearing maturity. This being granted, what constitutes religion is not the intellectual formulation of that consciousness; for this is properly the work of philosophy. But religion aims rather at expression in the language of the heart."

These definitions, good as far as they go, do not go far enough in distinguishing between the religious feelings and "an endeavor after a practical expression" of these feelings in acts of worship, or otherwise. Religious emotion is one thing; its "practical expression" is another. But it is enough for the purpose of these discourses to have shown (as is believed) that religion in its two chief elements of worship of God and a consciousness of immortality, has been shown by leading Evolutionists to have arisen early in the history of the human race, and grown with the growth of the Intellectual Powers, from low beginnings into its present manifestation among the most enlightened peoples.

It is not in accordance with the object of these discourses to examine any form of theology. Religion and theology will survive all changes in scientific doctrine, because they are based in fundamental elements of human character. Professor Le Seur (in *Popular Science Monthly* for May, 1887) says on this point: "Evolution is simply the current form of scientific opinion; we adhere to it because it seems to be the truth. Religion is that instinct in man which leads him to recognize and worship that which is highest and best. Far, then, from our submission to the truth cutting us off from religion, it should, and it will, bring religion nearer to us, and enable us some day to place it upon imperishable foundations, and to make it the abiding concentration of all thought and effort."

That the religious sentiments minister to the happiness of the race follows from the law of betterment admitted by the Evolutionists. Had they been more injurious than useful, they, and the races which held them in highest degree must have disappeared, and others with less religion must have survived them. But the contrary has been the fact in the history of the races, and those which have been most deeply religious have always been in the advance, other things being equal. And this has been true even without regard to the excellence or the want of it in the dominant party. For the religious feelings when they become intense kindle the ardor of all others, and make men brave, aggressive, and devoted to what is believed to be the divine cause, and generally successful against their less religious or fanatical enemies. Let us be thankful that ours is an age when the religious sentiments are more nearly emancipated from unmeaning Superstition than ever before, and our lot cast in a land where they are absolutely free to follow the teachings of the most enlightened intellect.

It is curious to note how, under this condition of unrestricted freedom, men are segregated from the mass who hold certain theological views in common, and are aggregated into separate congregations almost as numerous as unlimited divergence of views can demand. And the close observer will find that after making due allowance for the influence of early impressions, grades of "respectability" and a few other disturbing agencies, people are drawn into church relations by peculiarity of temperament, race, inheritance and other personal traits. So fully is this true that we can, in many cases, distinguish the sect with which men and women affiliate by knowing their personal peculiarities. One class goes to church A. They are calm, dignified, self-regarding, and generally well-to-do people, with questions of faith and conscience all settled. Another class belongs to church B. They permit no questions of conscience or creed, for both have been settled for them before they were born. They never neglect the mint and cummin, and walk by faith in their leaders. Class C is robust of mind, full of strong emotion, and not disposed to hide its expression; they are not deficient in faith, but are also disposed to work their passage to a Promised Land, and are ready to take everybody else with them. And so we might go through the alphabet of church aggregations, and not half exhaust the well marked varieties. But this is found to be held in common by nearly all of them: that Benevolence holds chief place among religious virtues;

and that "freedom to worship God" according to the dictates of individual conscience is the only assurance of heartfelt religion.

SERMON X.

"I am fearfully and wonderfully made."— Psalms cxxxix, 14.

Having in previous discourses attempted to show by the direct method that God reigns over, within and though the whole realm of nature, it is now proposed to proceed to the same end by the opposite road, especially as to the origin of man, and to find what was the work to be achieved by Evolution on the hypothesis of no God. In doing this it will not be assumed that Tyndall, Huxley, Spencer, Darwin, or any of the leading English Evolutionists hold Godless private opinions; though thousands of their followers in America not only hold that the universe exists without God, but they suppose themselves to be justified in so believing by the teachings of the authors named. Not so, however, with the eminent German author of the *History of Creation*. If the English translation of this really great work does Professor Haeckel no injustice, he teaches that man has been evolved by mechanical causes alone, under the influence of natural forces, without purpose, design, intention, or any guidance from any agency in the nature of intelligence. Starting from this assumption then, and for brevity's sake personifying Evolution, let us see what she undertook to do and what she has accomplished in the mechanical creation of man.

Starting with a speck of animated gelaton which came into existence no one knows how, and was the first of living things no one knows why, the problem was to make man of the dust of the earth—of such materials as she found ready at hand—and to fill him with the breath of life and all its concomitants.

Man was to stand upright. His framework was therefore necessarily rigid, tough and unyielding. Evolution made it of bone and made the bone. But bones were heavy and cumbersome; and so they were made hollow—putting the least material into the strongest form. They were also for equilibrium's sake made with bi-lateral symetry—right and left sides complementarily alike. And as bone is unyielding, and as the man was to have both motion and loco-motion, flexible joints were required at a hundred points. Evolution made all the joints; some hinge-like; some ball-and-socket; some (like the radius) rolling axially in grooves, and at every joint Evolution provided sacks of lubricating liquid to prevent friction, and saw to it that the sacks should carefully be kept full.

This bony skeleton was to be for support, for motion and loco-motion, and for the protection of tender parts. The brain and its appendages were to be safely housed in a bony cranium and down the central axis of the frame; accordingly the skull was made a hollow globe, arched on all sides, and its appended cord of nerve centre sent down the back in a cavity hollowed in the bony spine, while the spine itself, which contained and protected this precious cord, was carefully padded between all its many joints with elastic cartilages, to permit flexion and to prevent any violent shock which might work injury; and still further to secure this end, the bony column was given a double curvature, by which it might bend, and so lessen all shocks by its elasticity. And Evolution surveyed her work at this point, and saw that it was good.

But the eyes, and the ears, and all the special senses were to be in the cranium of unyielding bone ; and provision must be made for turning the head about without turning the whole body. Evolution—solely by mechanical means, without *intending* to do any such thing—provided a small opening in an upper vertebra of the spinal column, and fitted a pivot of bone into it for the revolution of the head, enabling it to revolve more perfectly than if design had wrought the mechanism by the hands of the most skillful artisan.

The next problem was—how this imprisoned brain and spinal marrow were to send their nerves out over the body, and to receive others in return. Here Evolution also worked much as an intelligent engineer would have done : she bored holes—foramins, anatomists call them—all down the spine for the passage of the nerves outward and inward ; and she did a similar work for the cranium, making a foraminal passage wherever it was needed for a nerve or a blood vessel to go out or in ; and she carefully made the foramins at the most convenient points. But all this was easy work—provided that Evolution had been permitted to think ; any carpenter could have done as much. She was to work without thought, and the next work on the skeleton, though still mechanical, was less the work of the carpenter and more that of the engineer. From the structure of the frame its movements were to be achieved at a loss of power, and the bony levers were to be moved by muscles acting nearer to the fulcrum than to the point of resistance. Evolution accordingly roughened the bones at numerous points for the better attachment of muscles, and threw out projecting spurs, protuberances and trochanters like those at the top of the thigh bones, the better to counteract the long end of the levers. If we were only permitted to attribute thought to Evolution, her skill in these contrivances which were not contrived, would appear wonderful. But it was all the mechanical result of blind forces.

The skeleton was also to furnish the framework of a pair of bellows, to supply the lungs with the breath of life: that wonderful mechanism called the chest was constructed, with all its hinges, braces and movable ribs; and no work of any skilled human inventor operates as well as that which came without invention.

And then the food grinding apparatus; a movable lower jaw so attached by hinges to a fixed upper one as to permit both a grinding movement from side to side, and a cutting movement up and down. There were also to be teeth, both cutters and grinders, and sockets were made in the jaws for these, and the cutting teeth inserted where least power was needed, and the grinders further back, as a wise workman would have planted them. But the teeth themselves really appear to have required some thought. Being from their structure incapable of increase in size after being once formed, and as those of childhood were too small for adult life, Evolution — equal to all emergencies — made two sets; one for childhood and the other to come later in life; even—as if knowing what would happen —preparing the second set at the roots of the first before these have completed their service.

But the skeleton was not yet complete. There must be an orifice on each side of the head where phonic vibrations of the air might be conveyed to the brain within, there to awaken the sensation of sound. Evolution made the orifices; and then she placed within the bony cavity of the ear a series of small, delicate and wonderfully appropriate compound levers of bone, to multiply the force of the vibratians. And all this without thought or any semblance of contrivance: it was only blind force finding its way at points of least resistance. It happened, curiously enough, that the work of making the "human machine" with two-sided symetry required two ears instead of one; which turned out very fortunately, as not only are we able to hear from either side, but if one ear is destroyed there may be a chance of hearing with the other.

The eyes were also to be provided for; and as they were to be globular, like a planet, and free to revolve, an orbit was formed for them under the projecting brow, for safety sake; and a small opening was made in the skull at the hinder part of the orbit to allow the passage of the optic nerve. These orbits are indeed remarkable uncontrived contrivances; but in this they are so far behind the eyes, which they were made for, that Evolution gets comparatively little credit for the sockets.

The organ of smell was also to be provided for; and this was by no means the least of the works undertaken and accomplished by Evolution. Not the external nose—that is simple enough—but the plan for spreading out a network of sensitive membrane in a very limited area. Imagine a fine sponge to have a delicate membrane spread out over its entire surface and lining all its tubes and cavities; that is what Evolution did for the "spongy bones," and as the air we breathe carries odorous particles through the channels of these spongy bones, and into contact with the sensitive membrane the sense of smell arises. And this was Evolution's work.

But we have already consumed half the space allowed to the skeleton, and are not half through with its wonders of mechanism—its braces, pullies, flexures, arches, cavities, cylinders and all that delicate internal structure of the bones known as their histogeny.

We have not considered the relations of the parts. But when it is remembered that Sir Charles Bell consumed an entire volume in treating of the structure and mechanism of the hand alone, it will be seen that the structures and adaptations of the entire body cannot even be enumerated in a single brief discourse.

And all this was the work of Evolution acting without intelligence on a living speck of gelatin! And if it is said—as justice demands—that Evolution has done nothing but recount the history of progression from the amœba to the man, then unconscious forces with the aid only of variation, survival of the fittest and heredity have evolved the human microcosm.

Is there any middle ground between this doctrine of evolution by unconscious physical forces acting mechanically, and that which assumes the immanency of Conscious Intelligence at work in all phenomena? Mr. J. J. Murphy, in his work on *Habit and Intelligence*, appears to think there is. He asserts his full belief in Evolution (which he calls development), but declares his belief " that some of the simplest structures belonging to the vegetable system have probably been produced by the action of inorganic forces upon the organism, and that muscular structure may possibly, though not probably, have been produced by the action of the organism itself in response to impressions from without. Of course these two factors are always both present, though acting in very enequal proportions in different cases. But there are structures for the origin of which it is, I believe," he continues, "impossible to account by any such merely physical theory, and which can only be referred to an organizing intelligence. I refer to such organs as the eye and the ear. If it is certain, as I think it is, that the flow of nutritive fluids through cellular tissue, for successive generations, must have a tendency to form a rudimentary circulating apparatus, it is at least equally obvious that the action of light falling on the eye for any number of generations can have no similar tendency to produce the optical apparatus of the eye." [Vol. I, p. 305].

Now it would appear that one who is ready to admit as Mr. Murphy does, that he thinks it certain "the flow of the nutritive fluids through cellular tissue for successive generations, must have a tendency to form a rudimentary circulating apparatus," and that the wonderful mechanism of the heart and arteries, veins and capillaries, arose in that way, should find no difficulty in admitting a similar origin to the eye. But Mr. Murphy thinks the eye was rather too much for the natural forces acting mechanically, and he falls back on what he calls "organizing intelligence" to account for the perfect eye. The Evolutionists point to the fact that the eye commenced as a mere spot of black paint, as in the eye of "the fish called the lancet (amphioxus), which is so simple" (as Darwin says) "that it consists only of a fold-like sack of skin, lined with pigment and furnished with a nerve, but destitute of any other apparatus, being merely covered by transparent membrane," and from that passed by mechanical forces through variation, survival of the fittest and heredity up to the eye of man. But Mr. Murphy replies that "no such merely physical theory will account for the origin of the special complexities of the visual apparatus." " Neither the action of light on the eye," he continues, " nor the action of the eye itself can have the slightest tendency to produce the wonderfully complex histological structure of the retina, nor to form the transparent humors of the eye into lenzes ; nor to produce the deposit of black pigment which absorbs the stray rays which would otherwise hinder clear vision ; nor to produce the iris, and endow it with the power of partly closing under a strong light so to protect the retina, and expanding again when the light is withdrawn ; nor to give the iris its two nervous connections, of which one has its root in the sympathetic ganglia, and causes expansion, while the other has its root in the brain, and causes contraction." Nevertheless, he thinks what he calls " *unconscious intelligence*" sufficient for even all this !

It is not to be understood that Mr. Murphy denies, or doubts, or even ignores the existence of a conscious God, for he does not ; but how such an admission is compatible with the doctrine of " unconscious organizing intelligence " does not appear. He declares that " formative or organizing intelligence is an

ultimate, inexplicable fact not capable of being resolved into any other." * * *
"Those who agree with me that the complexities of such organs as the eye and ear are due to unconscious intelligence, will probably feel no difficulty in believing the same of such wonderful motor instincts as the cell-building power of the bee and the wasp. [Vol, II, p. 1].

Now, after having declared that those complex organs and instincts are due to a "formative organizing intelligence," which "is an ultimate, inexplicable fact," why should Mr. Murphy add that this "fact" "is not resolvable into any other," when he himself admits the being of God? the only ultimate cause. Let us hope that the time is not far distant when men of science will no longer hesitate to admit in their writings (as most of them do in their hearts) that God reigns, the source, and sum, and substance of all science.

Rev. Canon Fremantle in an article published in the *Fortnightly Review*, quotes St. Augustine as saying: "God is unspeakable; yet what we say of Him would not be spoken at all if it were unspeakable. Even when we say God is unspeakable, we hardly speak rightly; for even in saying this we make an assertion. By pronouncing the word *Deus*, we do not make him known as He is. Only when that sound strikes the ears of men who know Latin, it moves in them the thought of a certain most excellent and immortal nature." [See *Popular Science Monthly*, June, 1887.]

What was it then which moved Herbert Spencer to invent the word *agnostic* as a name for those who do not admit Revelation, and believe that nothing can be known of God; and why is it thought necessary to avoid all mention of his name in nearly all recent works of science? Writers who do this do not hesitate to speak of gravity, or of the "universal ether," or of force and energy, of none of which is anything known, except their effects. Can it be sufficient reason for this agnosticism that the name of God (and of innumerable gods) has been the rallying cry of all religions and of all superstitions, even the most degraded? Hardly. The word *matter* has been subject to almost as great abuse as the name of God. Matter has been decried as vile, gross, dead and hateful; "a clog upon the soul;" and the material body as a 'prison-

GOD REIGNS 157

house, barring us from a better world," even by those who should know better. But scientific writers do not esteem matter as degraded thereby and hence decline to speak of it; but make that and its changes the burden of their thoughts. And yet they do not pretend to comprehend it. And even Mr. Spencer declares that "physical science is as little atheistic as it is materialistic." Canon Fremantle, in the paper already referred to, quotes Mr. Spencer as saying in the *Fortnightly Review*: "The student of Nature who starts from the axiom of the universality of the law of causation, cannot refuse to admit an eternal existence; if he admits the conservation of energy, he cannot deny the possibility of an eternal energy; if he admits the existence of immaterial phenomena in the form of consciousness, he must admit the possibility at any rate of an eternal series of such phenomena; and, if his studies have not been barren of the best fruit of the investigation of Nature, he will have enough sense to see that when Spinoza says, 'Per Deum intelligo ens absolute infinitum, hoc est substantiam constantem infinitis attributis,' the God so conceived is one that only a very great fool indeed would deny, even in his heart. Physical science is as little atheistic as it is materialistic."

If this be so—and certainly it is—might it not be well for this great thinker to devote a few pages now and then to the demonstration of the great truth that "physical science is as little atheistic as it is materialistic?" It would not be lost upon the thousands of non-scientific readers in this country who study his works and who believe that he teaches the contrary. Perhaps it is not too much to say that all Mr. Spencer's philosophy lacks of being the most complete and profound which has appeared among men, is the name of God.

SERMON XI.

"There is none other God but one; for though there be gods, that are called gods, whether in heaven or in earth (as there be gods many and lords many), but to us there is but one God, the Father, of whom are all things."—1 Cor.,VIII, 4-6.

The hypothesis of Evolution includes the following propositions, which will be the basis of discussion in the present discourse :

1. In the struggle for existence among plants and animals, the most favorably endowed in organic forms and functions survive, while the less fitted and unfitted ones perish.

2. In those variations in forms and functions which occur from whatever cause, useful ones beneficial to individuals and to associated members, tend to endure, and to increase from exercise; while injurious or useless ones decline or become extinct.

These propositions are true of man, as of

animals and plants; and held by all leading Evolutionists, and are fundamental.

Mr. Darwin says: "The new and improved forms of life tend to supplant the old and unimproved forms." [*Origin of Species*, § 512]. "We have every reason to believe that parent forms are generally supplanted and extinguished by their improved offspring.." [Id., p. 304]. "The theory of natural selection is grounded on the belief that each new variety, and ultimately each new species, is produced and maintained by having some advantage over those with which it comes in competition, and the consequent extinction of less favored forms almost inevitably follows." [Id., § 571.] Natural selection acts solely by the preservation of useful modifications [Id., § 756]; but we learn from the study of our domestic productions that the disuse of parts leads to their reduced size; and that the result is inherited." [Id., § 770.]

"And as natural selection works solely by and for the good of each being, all corporeal and mental endowments will tend to progress towards perfection." [Id., § 823.] And in his preface to the Second edition of the *Descent of Man,* Mr. Darwin says: " I may take this opportunity of remarking that my critics frequently assume that I attribute all changes of corporeal structure and mental power exclusively to the natural selection of such variations as are often called spontaneous; whereas, even in the first edition of the 'Origin of Species,' I distinctly stated that great weight must be attributed to the inherited effects of use and disuse, with respect to both the body and the mind." And in the sixth edition of the same work, as pointed out by Mr. Spencer in almost his latest work, entitled, " Factors of Organic Evolution," Mr. Darwin says : " I think there can be no doubt that use in our domestic animals has strengthened and enlarged certain parts, and disuse diminished them; and that such modifications are inherited." Returning to his work of the *Descent of Man,* Mr. Darwin says : " Changed structures which are in no way beneficial, cannot be kept uniform through natural selection, though the injurious will be thus eliminated. ' [§ 92.] " Owing to this struggle (for existence), variations, however slight and from whatever cause proceeding, if they be in any degree profitable to the individuals of a species in their infinitely complex relations to other organic beings and to their physical conditions of life, will tend to the preservation of such individuals, and will generally be inherited by the offspring." [§ 84.] "We may feel sure that any variation in the least degree injurious would be rigidly destroyed." [§ 109.]

And so throughout the writings of Mr. Darwin it is held that useful organic forms and functions tend to be preserved, while injurious ones decline and tend to become extinct. And it is believed that no other Evolutionist has expressed dissent from these views.

Speaking specially of the intellectual powers, Mr. Darwin says: "These faculties are variable, and we have every reason to believe that the variations tend to be inherited," [*Descent of Man*, § 210] and Mr. Spencer has taken pains to show that the brain and intellectual powers and emotions are subject to the same laws as the bodily structure and functions: these are preserved when useful, and when injurious disappear. And Mr. Darwin declares that the religious feelings have ministered to the advancement of the lower races, and their higher morality, in accordance with the same laws. [*Descent of Man*, § 251].

One remark from Mr. Spencer as to the evolution of structures and functions together, will conclude these citations from eminent Evolutionists as to the propositions assumed at the beginning of this discourse. "We have become quite familiar," he says, "with the idea of an evolution of structures throughout the ascending types of animals. To a considerable degree we have become familiar with the thought that an evolution of functions has gone on *pari passu* with the evolution of structures." [*Data of Ethics*, § 3.] And a large portion of Mr. Spencer's later work, "*The Factors of Organic Evolution*," is devoted to demonstration of "the doctrine that not only in the individual, but in the successions of individuals, use and disuse of parts produce respectively increase and decrease of them."

Now the history of the human race shows nothing more clearly than that the "ghost theory," (as Mr. Spencer calls it) and some form of the religious sentiment has been common to mankind in all countries, at all stages of progress, from the lowest savagism and the vilest fetichism to the most enlightened peoples and the most exalted religious sentiment to be found at the present day.

Dr. Fritze Schultze, in his exhaustive history of the rise, prevalence and evolution of fetichism, defines it as follows :

"By fetichism we understand the religious veneration of material objects. If such objects are to be worshipped they must first of all appear to be worthy of veneration, or, in other words, the worshipper must so consider them. The fetich, however, *e. g.*, a piece of metal, still continues to be in external form and in essential constitution, the self-same thing, whether observed by an European or an African. Hence, that which renders it a fetich is nothing intrinsic to the thing itself, but the view the fetichist takes of it. If, therefore we would understand fetichism in its true nature, we must investigate the savage's mode of apprehending the objects, or in other words, we must study the intellectual status of the fetichist. Fetichism has an historical position in all nations which stand lowest in intellectual development, that is, among savages so called. [Translated by J. Fitzgerald, p. 3].

By means of the accounts of travellers, memoirs of residence among savage races, narratives of missionaries and residents among rude tribes, and the published results of observation by many writers covering almost all tribes of rude, savage and barbarous people, he has shown the universal prevalence of fetichism in great variety among different tribes, and its essential agreement everywhere in being based on a conception of what Mr. Spencer calls "the ghost theory," the origin of which he accounts for as shown in a previous discourse.

Here, then, is the case of a trait of human character which originated in the very night and darkness of the race, became organized in the brain, and has been transmitted by inheritance through many generations, rising through all forms of fetichism, ancestor-worship, sun-worship, and all the phases of polytheism to the highest conception of the most advanced believers in that "one God, the

Father," of whom Paul wrote to the Corinthians. Nor does it detract at all from this high conception to remember through what by-ways of superstition men have reached an upper plane of religious faith and feeling; for the moral sentiments of justice, benevolence, truthfulness and all the elements of a pure morality have come up in the same way by slow advances from very low beginnings. Is religion in itself, then, devoid of theological doctrines, unworthy the consideration of Evolutionists, that they should disregard it in their laborious researches into the evolution of the race? And if it be evil, why, then, has it not long ago perished from the earth, in accordance with the declared laws of Evolution? Why have tribes and peoples with deepest religious impulses been "selected" to survive? No other strong trait can be shown to have begun earlier, been more nearly universal, and persisted in the structure of the brain as a constantly manifested function than the religious feelings. Must not that be good for the race which has survived so long? If it were not, the fundamental laws of Evolution should have exterminated it long ago.

Professor Le Sueur, one of the foremost of American Evolutionists, takes note of this survival of the religious " instinct " (as he calls it), and in *Popular Science Monthly* for May, 1887, says: "Evolution is simply the current form of scientific opinion. We adhere to it because it seems to be the truth. Religion is that instinct in man which leads him to recognize and worship that which is highest and best. Far, then, from our submission to the truth cutting us off from religion, it should and it will, bring religion nearer to us, and make us some day to place it upon imperishable foundations, and to make it the abiding consecration of all thought and effort." [Page 39.]

It may be asked: Why should it have been necessary for those religious sentiments which now play so important a part in the nature of man and bring him into conscious relation to the Father-God as conceived by the most exalted minds, to have begun in such base superstitions as the thousand forms of fetichism, and to have passed through mental darkness and bloody rites, up to that conception and life which were manifested in Jesus of Nazareth? The question is perfectly pertinent. But it involves that other and broader question: Why did civilized and enlightened man start as an ignorant savage? Even now, in this exalted age which exultantly looks down on forty centuries of comparative ignorance, how few have an enlightened conception of what Mr. Spencer was pleased to characterize as "the ghost theory?" Evolutionists, at least, cannot complain of the long ages of advancement which have been necessary to bring men to such a conception of that "theory" as shall lead them to do justly, and to love mercy, and to walk humbly with God.

The ghost theory must have involved the greatest usefulness to the race, to have survived its long night of savagery and barbarism to the present time. Moreover, the "religious instinct," as Professor Le Sueur calls it, has swayed mankind as a ruling impulse in his passage from savagery to civilization as no other has. And if "no race has been lifted out of barbarism without the aid of supernatural machinery," as declared by Mr. Burroughs, in a paper entitled "The Natural versus the Supernatural" [*Popular Science Monthly*, May, 1887], it follows that it must have constantly worked out the welfare of the race; for all injurious organic forms and functions—in the brain as elsewhere—perish. The religious sentiments — the functional manifestations of organic forms in the brains of a thousand generations — have survived all "struggle for existence," and so proved their value to mankind; and it cannot be presumptious to assume that they will survive the neglect of agnosticism, the direct attacks of atheism and the indirect assaults of exclusive materialism. But in making this declaration it is no more necessary to define this persistent element of human character by some specific theological dogma than it was that Mr. Spencer, in his work on the Data of Ethics, should have formulated a code of morals. If the ethical sentiments and practices which prevail among the most highly advanced persons of the present day arose from such barbarous beginnings as shown by Mr. Spencer, and have passed upward through ages of evolution; and if at each stage of progress the prevailing ethics was that best suited to its people, there can be no reason to doubt that the successively prevailing religious sentiments and rites of every age and people have been—all things considered—the best. And it only remains for some devout Evolutionist to do for religion what Mr. Spencer has done for ethics.

The conclusion will no doubt be that men in a state of barbarism were no more able to conceive and be moved by the highest religious motives than by the highest ethics. Even Jesus, the exemplar for all mankind, said to his special followers at one time: " I have yet many things to say unto you, but ye cannot bear them now." [John xvi, 12.] And at various other times he intimated to his disciples that they were not yet able to bear the whole truth. His apostle, Paul, said to the Corinthians: " I have fed you with milk and not meat; for hitherto ye were not able to bear it; neither yet now are ye able, for ye are yet carnal." [1 Cor., iii, 2-3.] And while religion pertains to the emotions and affections, which are blind and do not reason, and have grown up as feelings, all theologies, which belong to the reasoning powers, but are equally with the feelings manifested through the brain, must necessarily have also had their rise in gross intellectual darkness in the infancy of the race, and have come up through much tribulation to their highest expression.

It is not forgotten that religion and morality are so intimately related as to be frequently confounded and treated as one ; but while religion involves "that instinct in man which leads him to recognize and worship that which is highest and best," morality is more properly confined to man's relations with his fellow man. And both, if either, have risen by slow variations from a very low to a much higher degree of usefulness and excellence.

It is not to be supposed that Evolutionists have overlooked the momentous part which the religious feelings have played in the history of mankind. Why, then, have they so generally failed to give them due attention ? Is it not that agnosticism has become a creed among the chief expounders of the new philosophy, and they therefore decline to treat of what is or may be known, because they do not know more ? But creeds in science are at least as hurtful as they are sometimes in religion. Professor Huxley, in his address at the unveiling of a statue of Darwin, declared that "science commits suicide when it adopts a creed." But the agnosticism which declares that nothing can be known of God is as truly a creed, though a negation, as any positive declaration of theology. Moreover, it is a creed which has, comparatively speaking, but few earnest followers. Let it be admitted that scientific research can determine nothing as to the existence and attributes of God beyond their manifestations in the phenomena of the universe. The same is true of gravitation and all force and energy, of the universal ether, of self-consciousness, and of other things, to the study of which agnosticism offers no bar. And even if nothing at all can be known of God, none know better than Mr. Spencer and the Evolutionists that man in all stages of his advancement has been swayed by that ghost theory which includes both spirit existence and immortality beyond temporal death. That is therefore as worthy of the profound study of scientific observers as is biology, sociology or ethics. And if there is nothing spiritual or immaterial to which the ghost theory bears relation ; if Evolution has organized a lie in the human brain which has survived through all generations, then the Evolutionist who shall demonstrate that will have written his name high up in the temple of science, and may henceforth rest upon his laurels.

SERMON XII.

"He that built all things is God."—Hebrews III, 4.

To any one who has followed these discourses it is hardly necessary to say that the chief object in them has been to support the declaration of Professor Tyndall, that "*it is no departure from scientific method to place behind natural phenomena a universal Father, who, in answer to the prayers of His children, alters the currents of those phenomena.*" Nevertheless, it has not been attempted to show that the universal Father ever does "alter the currents" of natural phenomena; but that being immanent—in-dwelling—in all things and with perfect knowledge without having to reason in search of it, there can be no possible necessity at any time to make any change in the currents of natural phenomena.

In supporting this proposition almost exclusive consideration has been given to that wide-reaching philosophy of modern days which bears the name of Evolution ; because that hypothesis as now understood comprehends the whole range of phenomena appreciable to the human consciousness. If God be excluded from evolution, there can be no place for him in all his boundless universe.

Nor has the truth of the doctrine as taught by its ablest expounders been directly questioned. Evolution is a fact as well ascertained as gravitation ; but what is its extent and what are its limitations remain to be determined by evolutionists themselves. But all indications from the imperfections in the doctrine as taught by the most advanced Evolutionists, and many avowals made by them, tend to prove that it can never be complete until God shall be restored as the conscious center and bond of unity for the whole system of philosophy. It is not claimed by its teachers that Evolution is either itself a force or the sum of many forces; but only that it is a scientific account of those phenomena by which matter has reached the present condition of the material universe, and especially of that portion which we know as organic.

Since the previous discourses of this series were prepared, there has come to hand a remarkable lecture upon the same subject, from which a few paragraphs will be cited as showing how one of America's ablest naturalists and Evolutionists—Professor E. D. Cope— looks upon the philosophy which ignores the existence of God, and teaches that organization is the cause of life and consciousness. Speaking of the difficulty of treating the question scientifically, Professor Cope says that "this difficulty is increased by the fact that a majority of scientific men avoid the subject; * * * and they either look for light to the future exclusively, or they avoid it altogether, or treat it with considerable inhospitality, to say the least." [*Theology and Evolution*; Arnold & Co., Philadelphia, p. 4.] Of consciousness he declares that "it is not only entirely distinct in its essential nature from matter, but it is also totally distinct from energy and motion. The whole universe and all phenomena in it are expressed in the three words. Matter, tridimentional, is the basis. Energy is the motion of that matter. Thirdly, consciousness is the mind which some of that matter exhibits. These are three totally independent, distinct, uncommingleable, absolutely and essentially different subjects of thought." [P. 17.] "If we go back to the very simplest animal, a drop of jelly known as the amœba, we find that these very small beings display some mental qualities in a rudimental condition without any structure at all worth mentioning; so it is evident that *consciousness was there first*, and the structure came afterwards, through activity." [P. 24.] Professor Cope then proceeds to show that in the evolution of animal forms, up to the highest evolution, was in the activity of the animals from their own volition ; every act was a designed act, "and their own design runs through them all." "We get from this history," he says, "further proof of the control of mind over matter; for the capacity of animals or living things to create their own organs, in accordance with their own immediate necessities, and thus to enable themsèlves to acquire their modes of life as we find them today, is clearly an evidence of this power. Thus science proves that mind is the creator of organisms, under the conditions furnished by the environment. This is the first step in evidence of the existence of a great mind, since the lesser minds must have been derived from some common source like the structures which display them." [P. 25.]

And after a pretty full consideration of the whole matter, he declares as to the scientific evidence for the existence of God as follows: "The demonstration of the primitive function of mind, so far as it has gone, must be of the greatest possible interest and the greatest possible service to persons who perceive its wide bearing. There are some persons who do not care for that sort of demonstration. Perhaps they are happy. I would not interfere with the happiness of that man who is satisfied without the privilege of knowing the truth. For my own part I have occasion to be extremely grateful that I live in a time when the evidence for such truth is accessible. Although some parts of the argument have not been unknown to some of the best theologians—it has not been in such shape as to constitute a demonstration, nor in a state to be acceptable to science; it has been made provable and nothing more. But when it comes to take the form of an absolute proposition with certain demonstration, we have done what Job said could not be done, namely, by searching we have found out God. Job's expression is very correct, provided it means that you connot touch, see or handle the Supreme Being by searching with the ordinary senses of the body. And this is a rational way in which we may apprehend his Being and believe in Him; and the consequences of such understanding must be to increase our belief in the stability of the universe, and in our own chances of a future life." [Page 28.]

There are certain facts of organic evolution which are not accounted for in the hypothesis of Mr. Darwin, or of other Evolutionists. Some of these are:

1. From the very beginning, as before indicated, it has been impossible to account for those "few simple living forms," from which all living organisms since are claimed to have sprung. They could not have arisen spontaneously; that implies the rise of the living from the not-living, without a reason for it; though Professor Haeckel and others believe that we are compelled by the logic of Evolu-

tion to make that assumption. They cannot be claimed to have arisen fortuitously, for this is contrary to established scientific principles. Moreover, the specks of "protoplasm," in which life first "arose" have not themselves been accounted for. "How was the first protoplasm created?" asks Professor Cope [page 25]. "We have seen that plants manufacture protoplasm and other organic substances out of inorganic matter. * * * But protoplasm is necessary to the process. Whence, then, was the first protoplasm derived?" [Page 26.]

2. No sufficient reason has been shown for that uniform tendency to improvement and the rise to a condition of betterment, which is seen in both inorganic, and especially in organic nature. In truth, there is no reason at all shown by evolution without God, why there should be an organized universe, and *why there should be any evolution in it.*

3. Those "variations" of the organism by which "the fittest survive" in the struggle for existence, remain to be accounted for. "And these useful variations fortuitously arising," as Mr. Spencer calls them in his latest work—

"*Factors of Organic Evolution*" [page 37]—which are inheritable, come in opposition to the law of inheritance according to which the offspring should be like the progenitors. And of this very thing Mr. Spencer says in the same work: "Supposing all to agree that from the beginning, along with inheritance of useful variations fortuitously arising, there has been inheritance of effects produced by use and disuse; do there remain no classes of organic phenomena unaccounted for? To this question I think it must be replied that there do remain classes of phenomena unaccounted for." [Page 37,] Where, then, is the real source of these organic phenomena which "remain unaccounted for?" As a suggestion of the answer to this inquiry, read the closing paragraph of Professor Cope's lecture, before quoted from:

"The evidence which sustains a belief in a great Mind now invisible to us, and in a possible future life, is based on the knowledge that we possess of the control of mind over matter. This is derived from three sources: First, from the design displayed by the energy of living things; second, from the control by living over chemical energy; third, from the directive power of mind over the process of Evolution.

4. Evolution does not account for the happiness to which it tends in the advancement of all animal organisms. Mr. Spencer's explanation is not sufficient. He says: " Pains are the correlatives of actions injurious to the organism, while pleasures are the correlatives of actions conducive to its welfare;" since " it is an inevitable deduction from the hypothesis of Evolution that the races of sentient creatures could have come into existence under no other conditions." [*Principles of Psychology*, §124.] This only states a fact (if it be a fact), but does not account for it. Why does the economy of animate existence demand that it must result in happiness, or must not exist at all? And why must it exist at all, if there be no loving Father-God, " that built all things ?" It might possibly be shown that—given matter and force—a solar system and an inorganic world must have come into existence. But even Evolutionists will scarcely claim that races of animated creatures conditioned upon their happiness

must necessarily have peopled that world.
As to the deficiencies of the doctrine of Evolution as it now stands, Mr. Spencer closes a discussion of them by saying : "Whatever may be thought of the arguments and conclusions set forth in this article and the preceding one, they will perhaps serve to show that it is as yet far too soon to close the inquiry concerning the causes of organic Evolution." [*Factors of Organic Evolution*, 1886, p. 75.]

Mr. Spencer is right ; " it is far too soon to close the inquiry." It will not be safe to assume that it is closed until it has been considered that God reigns in Evolution as he is supreme in the universe.

A brief summary of the points sought to be established in these discourses will bring them to a close.

For necessity, in making quotations and referring to the language of others, the word "spirit" has been used. But it is not assumed (nor denied) that it is something "supernatural ; " or that it is "an intelligence conceived of apart from any physical organization or embodiment." That involves a subordinate question to be settled by itself.

In the same manner the word "*supernatural*" has been avoided as involving another subordinate question. Professor Cope prefers the word "supersensuous," which, as he says, "some people call the supernatural, * * * because all is in accordance with our system of laws, which we call natural laws."

In accordance with the views maintained in these discourses, all is natural or all is supernatural; God is alike in all and over all. And it is consistent to hold that the same body of laws (speaking figuratively) holds good throughout all worlds. And of those laws, and of that which we personify as *Nature,* wherein the so-called laws are manifested, Mr. Darwin has this to say: " I have also often personified the word nature, but I mean by nature only the aggregate action and product of many natural laws—and by laws only the ascertained sequence of events." [*Animals and Plants Under Domestication, Introduction*, p. 6.] Let us go one step further back, and call that which Mr. Darwin here calls "the ascertained sequence of events" the manifestations to our consciousness of that infinite Consciousness, the cause of all phenomena, "who built all things."

But though God through phenomena becomes manifest to our consciousness, it must be under the same restrictions and in the same manner in which we are conscious of the material world, and of that all we can know is its effect upon consciousness itself. Of what matter is "in itself" we can know nothing. But the same must be true of all that is near and dear to us—wife, children and friends, and the loving and beloved who are the objects of those strong affections which warm and vivify all our social relations. And in the same manner the devout worshipper is moved by a profound consciousness of that loving Father who, as the apostle declares, is not far from each one of us; standing not apart from his works and surveying as at a distance the phenomena which he commands, but everywhere present in loving kindness to care for His conscious creatures; not permitting the universe to move as an infinite machine from its own mechanism, but at all times controlling its phenomena by the counsels of his own will;

issuing no "laws" for the government of material things, but exerting his own volition in infinite wisdom at all times; permitting no "catastrophies" to befall his works, but controlling all apparent discord to compel a universal harmony—that is the thought of God which arises in the consciousness and finds a devout response in every sufficiently intelligent being who has not preferred darkness rather than light.

And now, does it not appear that any other conclusion would involve an anti-climax so prodigious as to convict that Nature which could be supposed to exist without God of infinite folly? Setting out in the puerile ignorance of primeval man, the outcome of countless ages of organic evolution, shadows, echoes, images and dreams awaken the wondering savage with the *ghost theory*. Long ages of evolution through innumerable and indescribable fetichisms elevate mankind through ancestor-worship, star-worship and sun-worship—through lords many and gods many—to a dim conception of that one God whose essence is Love; when lo! Evolution abandons its greatest work, ignores God, and self-convicted of infinite folly, sinks to an absurd anti-climax. And if not that, at least declines to follow to the end for the long-sought consummation to which all change and all advancement have tended.

www.ingramcontent.com/pod-product-compliance
Lightning Source LLC
Chambersburg PA
CBHW032147160426
43197CB00008B/806